GALATIANS:

DISPENSATIONALLY CONSIDERED

A GRACE EXPOSITIONAL COMMENTARY

SECOND EDITION

Steven L. Tackett

Compiled and edited by:

Dr. David Alan Greene

Contents

To Grace Believers everywhere —

one in the Body of Christ

But I certify you, brethren,
that the gospel which was preached of me
is not after man.
For I neither received it of man,
neither was I taught it,
but by the revelation of Jesus Christ.

– The Apostle Paul

Acknowledgements

I would like to express my gratitude to my beloved wife Stephanie. She has been a constant source of support and encouragement to me. A special thanks to Dave Greene, my brother in Christ, who compiled and edited this book.

To the reader, it is my sincere hope and prayer that this book will bring you to a deeper understanding of the Gospel of Grace. It stands alone in this current dispensation. Remember this. We are saved by grace through faith and not of works (Eph. 2:8). Anything that we add to achieve or maintain our salvation diminishes what Christ has already done for us on the Cross. We are saved by grace alone through the finished work of Jesus Christ's death, burial, and resurrection. Salvation is ours when we believe that what Jesus has done for us is sufficient. To this, we can add nothing!

Introduction

It is the purpose of this book to go through the book of Galatians verse by verse. However, before we get into the text, we need to cover some preliminary ground. Some readers may not be familiar with the biblical concept of *apostleship*. Since this is critical for the understanding of this book, let us take a moment to examine this.

In the role of *apostle*, Paul is specifically appointed to carry a unique message to designated recipients. We will start by looking at what it means to be an *apostle* by asking this question: *What are the qualifications to be an apostle?* For the answer, let us look at Acts 9:1-2:

> 1 **And Saul, yet breathing out threatenings and slaughter against the disciples of the Lord, went unto the high priest, 2 And desired of him letters to Damascus to the synagogues, that if he found any of this way,**

whether they were men or women,
he might bring them bound unto Jerusalem.

There is a watershed moment in Acts 8. We are
first introduced to Saul of Tarsus. Up until this point
he had never been mentioned in the Bible. This man
will later become the Apostle Paul. Prior to that, we
see him breathing out "threatenings" against Jesus'
followers. Verses 3-6:

> 3 And as he journeyed, he came near
> Damascus: and suddenly there
> shined round about him a light from
> heaven: 4 And he fell to the earth,
> and heard a voice saying unto him,
> Saul, Saul, why persecutest thou me?

> 5 And he said, Who art thou, Lord?
> And the Lord said, I am Jesus whom
> thou persecutest: it is hard for thee to
> kick against the pricks. 6 And he
> trembling and astonished said, Lord,
> what wilt thou have me to do? And
> the Lord said unto him, Arise, and go
> into the city, and it shall be told thee
> what thou must do.

Notice his fellow travelers were witnesses to

this event. Verse 7:

> 7 **And the men which journeyed with him stood speechless, hearing a voice, but seeing no man.**

Saul, with great determination, sought to pursue the followers of the Kingdom Gospel. As a result, he has an encounter with the resurrected and glorified Lord Jesus Christ. He was blinded and fell to the ground in this divine confrontation. Verses 8-9:

> 8 **And Saul arose from the earth; and when his eyes were opened, he saw no man: but they led him by the hand, and brought him into Damascus. 9 And he was three days without sight, and neither did eat nor drink.**

Saul was completely helpless and his mind must have been spinning. As a devout Jew, a Pharisee, he was completely familiar with the teachings of Almighty God according to the Old Testament Scriptures. On that day God spoke directly to him just as He did with Moses. Verses 10-16:

> 10 **And there was a certain disciple at Damascus, named Ananias; and to him said the Lord in a vision,**

Ananias. And he said, Behold, I am here, Lord.

11 And the Lord said unto him, Arise, and go into the street which is called Straight, and enquire in the house of Judas for one called Saul, of Tarsus: for, behold, he prayeth, 12 And hath seen in a vision a man named Ananias coming in, and putting his hand on him, that he might receive his sight.

13 Then Ananias answered, Lord, I have heard by many of this man, how much evil he hath done to thy saints at Jerusalem: 14 And here he hath authority from the chief priests to bind all that call on thy name.

15 But the Lord said unto him, <u>Go thy way: for he is a chosen vessel unto me, to bear my name before the Gentiles, and kings, and the children of Israel</u>: 16 For I will shew him how great things he must suffer for my name's sake.

Now, the Lord appeared to Saul of Tarsus and

it would be the Lord Who would make him His
Apostle. In the opening to Galatians, we see the statement concerning his credentials. Galatians 1:1:

1 **Paul, an apostle, (not of men, neither by man, but by Jesus Christ, and
God the Father, who raised him from
the dead;)**

Paul begins by making this important point. He is an
Apostle appointed by the risen Lord. He was not or-
dained by men nor was he self-appointed. He was
made an Apostle by direct appointment from the resurrected and glorified Lord Jesus Christ Himself.

Let us consider this. Romans 11:13:

13 **For I speak to you Gentiles, inas-
much as I am the apostle of the Gentiles, I magnify mine office:**

Paul is very clear. On the road to Damascus, while
seeking to persecute the followers of the Kingdom
message, the Lord Jesus Christ confronted Paul face
to face. Again, He appointed him to be His Apostle
to the Gentiles.

One may ask, "What does the word apostle
mean?" In Greek, the original language in which the

New Testament was written, the word *apostolos* simply means "messenger" or "one who is sent." It also carries with it that the sender has a message. For Paul's case, God tells Ananias that He appointed him "to bear my name before the Gentiles, and kings, and the children of Israel" (Acts 9:15). These are the ones to whom Paul's message is sent.

Every believer is called to share this Gospel with others. However, to be sent as an apostle is different. It carries a very special appointment and directs the apostle to a specific recipient. The Lord Jesus Christ appointed Peter James, John, and the other apostles. Their ministry and message were specific as well. He appointed the Twelve to bring the Gospel of the Kingdom to the lost sheep of Israel. Their message was different from Paul's. These are the Twelve who were chosen by the Lord during His earthly ministry. He gave them instructions to bring their message to specific recipients. Matthew 10:5:

> 5 **These twelve Jesus sent forth, and commanded them, saying, <u>Go not into the way of the Gentiles, and into any city of the Samaritans enter ye not:</u>**

Again, the Twelve were appointed as apostles for a specific purpose. They are *not* to go to the Gentiles, but rather go to the house of Israel! Verses 6-7:

> **6 But <u>go rather to the lost sheep of the</u>
> <u>house of Israel</u>.**
>
> **7 And as ye go, preach, saying, <u>The</u>**
> **<u>kingdom of heaven is at hand</u>.**

Jesus' instructions are clear. They have a very specific ministry and it is only to the lost sheep of Israel; not to the Gentiles. Furthermore, it is the Gospel of the Kingdom. This good news was that Israel's Messiah, their future King, was at hand and ready to establish the Kingdom promised to their fathers. (See Rom. 15:8.)

Let us consider Christ's offices for Israel. Hebrews 3:1:

> **1 Wherefore, holy brethren, partak-**
> **ers of the heavenly calling, consider**
> **the Apostle and High Priest of our**
> **profession, Christ Jesus;**

Above we have a reference to the Lord Jesus Christ using two titles: *Apostle* and *High Priest*. Is it possible to hold more than one office? Why is there a reference to Christ Himself as being an Apostle? The reason is that He was One sent by God the Father to complete a very specific task. He was sent with a specific message to a designated recipient—"the lost sheep of Israel." After His resurrection, Christ intercedes as Israel's High Priest. This was a very special appointment made by God Himself. The Temple will be destroyed in 70 AD. In heaven, Christ currently continues to intercede between the children of Israel and God.

Let us turn to Acts 26. Here, Paul is speaking in front of King Agrippa. He is telling the King about the events that took place at his meeting with the resurrected Christ (See Acts 9:1-22). Here, we learn more details about what the Lord Jesus Christ communicated to Paul in that meeting. Acts 26:13-18:

> 13 **At midday, O king, I saw in the way a light from heaven, above the brightness of the sun, shining round about me and them which journeyed with me.**
>
> 14 **And when we were all fallen to the earth, I heard a voice speaking unto me, and saying in the Hebrew tongue, Saul, Saul, why persecutest thou me? it is hard for thee to kick against the pricks.**

15 And I said, Who art thou, Lord? And he said, I am Jesus whom thou persecutest.

16 But rise, and stand upon thy feet: for I have appeared unto thee for this purpose, to make thee a minister and a witness both of these things which thou hast seen, and of those things in the which I will appear unto thee;

17 Delivering thee from the people, and from the Gentiles, unto whom now I send thee,

18 To open their eyes, and to turn them from darkness to light, and from the power of Satan unto God, that they may receive forgiveness of sins, and inheritance among them which are sanctified by faith that is in me.

Here we see the *apostleship* of Paul in greater detail. We can see notable differences between the message entrusted to him and the message entrusted to the Twelve. Those differences are both in the message itself and the intended recipients. We saw the message of the Twelve is to preach that the Kingdom was at hand. Their message was to be directed only to "the lost sheep of the house of Israel." However, in the passage we just read, we see that Paul's message was to be sent to the Gentiles and any Jews who accept the message of the Grace of God.

For clarification, the word *Gentiles* means *non-Jews*. It is derived from the Hebrew word *Goyim* which means *nations*. The nations were created when all the people on earth were scattered at the Tower of Babel. (See Genesis 11:1-9.) As a result of the scattering, the people became many nations with different languages. In Genesis 12, Abram was called out of the many nations for the purpose of becoming a separate, or *holy*, nation dedicated to God. Therefore, the Jews were separated from all other nations because of God's singular calling. We will see other references in the Bible to *non-Jews* with words used like *heathen* or *the uncircumcision*. This is important to remember as we move through the book of Galatians.

Let us continue with our examination of the title *apostle*. 1 Corinthians 1:1:

1 Paul, called to be <u>an apostle of Jesus Christ through the will of God</u> . . .

In Paul's other letters, we will find the words *grace* and *peace* used in the salutation. Why? It is because his message has two important aspects. Paul's message is all about the *grace* of God being extended to the Gentiles. It is also about *peace* with God as He withholds His judgment on sin during the Age of Grace. Romans 1:1:

> 1 **Paul, a servant of Jesus Christ, <u>called to be an apostle, separated unto the gospel of God,</u>**

Paul continues his greeting. Verse 7:

> 7 **To all that be in Rome, beloved of God, called to be saints: <u>Grace to you and peace from God our Father, and the Lord Jesus Christ.</u>**

Let us turn to the Gospel of John. I would like to make another important point about what it means to be an apostle in general. John 13:20:

> 20 **Verily, verily, I say unto you, He that receiveth whomsoever I send receiveth me; and he that receiveth me receiveth him that sent me.**

Paul was sent by Christ just as the other apostles were. Apostleship is a very unique office when sent by God. Whatever the message is, it is being sent directly from the One Who is sending it. It comes with the full authority of the Sender. The recipients of the message are to accept it as coming from God Himself. According to the Lord, receiving an apostle's message is equal to receiving it from Him. Although the apostles are mere mortals, their message must not be discounted, criticized, or rejected. It is important to understand the significance of the messages being delivered.

Look again at the Gospel of John where we read the prayer that the Lord Jesus Christ prayed on behalf of His Twelve. John 17:17-18:

> **17 Sanctify them through thy truth: thy word is truth. 18 As thou hast sent me into the world, even so have I also sent them into the world.**

This prayer is *not* about the Church–the Body of Christ. It is *not* about the world. It is about Kingdom Believers. Verses 19-22:

> **19 And for their sakes I sanctify myself, that they also might be sanctified through the truth. 20 Neither pray I for these alone, but for them also which shall believe on me through their word;**

21 That they all may be one; as thou, Father, art in me, and I in thee, that they also may be one in us: that the world may believe that thou hast sent me. 22 And the glory which thou gavest me I have given them; that they may be one, even as we are one:

Again, the sending of an apostle is the same as sending the Christ. They are His authorized representatives here on earth. It is for this reason that no one can be a self-appointed apostle. Those who call themselves an apostle are guilty of serious misrepresentation. Apostles must be appointed directly by the One they represent, the Lord Jesus Christ Himself. They carry the message given directly to them by Him. The message given to Peter, James, and John and the other apostles is different from the message given to Paul—even though they are all apostles.

Let us look at the Gospel of Luke. This event occurs after the resurrection of Christ. He is explaining to His Apostles why these things must have taken place. Pay particular attention to these words: *repentance* and *remission of sins*. Luke 24:44-48:

44 And he said unto them, These are the words which I spake unto you, while I was yet with you, that all

things must be fulfilled, which were written in the law of Moses, and in the prophets, and in the psalms, concerning me.

45 Then opened he their understanding, that they might understand the scriptures, 46 And said unto them, Thus it is written, and thus it behoved Christ to suffer, and to rise from the dead the third day:

47 And <u>that repentance and remission of sins should be preached</u> in his name among all nations, beginning at Jerusalem. 48 And ye are witnesses of these things.

They did not understand the prophecies in the Old Testament that their Messiah must be crucified and rise from the dead. They did not know until Christ explained it to them. These things must happen to fulfill all that was written about Him. Now, they understood.

The above verses use the words *repentance* and *remission of sins*. This is the message they are to preach in His name. They are to preach it among all the nations for the *putting aside of their sins*. However, the forgiveness of their sins are deferred until the Second Coming when they will have their sins forgiven. Until then, they are to preach the Gospel of the Kingdom to all nations beginning at Jerusalem. We will look at another verse. After His resurrection and prior to His ascension, Jesus is speaking to His Apostles. Acts 1:8:

> 8 But ye shall receive power, after that the Holy Ghost is come upon you: and <u>ye shall be witnesses unto me both in Jerusalem, and in all Judaea, and in Samaria, and unto the uttermost part of the earth.</u>

Here is the order of His instructions to them: (1) preach the Gospel of the Kingdom as they did in Matthew, Mark, Luke, and John starting in Jerusalem, (2) move outward from Jerusalem to Judaea and Samaria, and (3) bring that message of the Kingdom to the farthest reaches of the earth. His instructions seem pretty clear. However, there was a problem.

When we read Acts 8, we see that the Apostles never got out of Jerusalem due to the great persecution. Then, God temporarily suspended the Age of Law. It will resume at the end of the Age of Grace and the beginning of the Tribulation which will be the final testing of true Israel. Paul's message is to the

Gentiles. Ephesians 3:1-7:

> 1 **For this cause I Paul, the prisoner of Jesus Christ for you Gentiles, 2 If ye have heard of <u>the dispensation of the grace of God</u> which is given me to you-ward:**
>
> 3 **How that by revelation he made known unto me the mystery; (as I wrote afore in few words, 4 Whereby, when ye read, ye may understand my knowledge in the mystery of Christ) 5 Which in other ages was not made known unto the sons of men, as it is now revealed unto his holy apostles and prophets by the Spirit;**
>
> 6 **That the Gentiles should be fellow-heirs, and of the same body, and partakers of his promise in Christ by the gospel: 7 Whereof I was made a minister, according to the gift of the grace of God given unto me by the effectual working of his power.**

What is this Gospel of the Grace of God? Paul defines it for us. 1 Corinthians 15:1-4:

1 Moreover, brethren, I declare unto you the gospel which I preached unto you, which also ye have received, and wherein ye stand; 2 By which also ye are saved, if ye keep in memory what I preached unto you, unless ye have believed in vain.

3 For I delivered unto you first of all that which I also received, <u>how that [1] Christ died for our sins according to the scriptures; 4 And that he [2] was buried, and that [3] he rose again the third day according to the scrip-tures</u>:

This is the unique message that the Apostle Paul was commissioned to preach. It is *not* the same as the Gospel of the Kingdom preached by the Twelve Apostles! And, this is how the Gospel of Grace works. Ephesians 2: 8-9:

8 For by grace are ye saved through faith; and that not of yourselves: it is the gift of God: 9 Not of works, lest any man should boast.

The message Christ gave to Paul is that He died for our sins, was buried, and rose again the third day.

The work of salvation was completed. What should be our response? Our response should be one of faith. We should believe that Christ has done it all. Salvation is available to everyone, but only applies to those who believe. There is nothing that needs to be done. Anything we do to earn our salvation is considered "works." We must have faith by believing that Christ died for our sins, was buried, and rose again the third day. That, my friends, is the Gospel of Grace!

Christ commissioned Paul to be an Apostle and this is the message He gave to Paul. Changing His gospel, in any way, makes it "another" gospel. That is what was happening within the assemblies in Galatia. The message of grace they received from Paul was being altered. They were mixing grace with the Law. They were adding elements of the Mosaic Law into the Gospel of Grace. Today, many churches, in the same manner, combine grace with the Law.

This situation is what moved Paul to write to the Galatians. They initially had believed Paul's message of the Gospel of Grace. There were religious Jews who came in among the Galatians and insisted on also keeping the Law. They convinced the people that salvation was by grace plus works. They were telling them that to be saved, they must believe the

Gospel of Grace and also keep the commandments. This is the issue Paul addresses in his letter to the Galatians.

1

Galatians 1

Let us start with Galatians 1:1-2:

1 Paul, an apostle, (not of men, neither by man, but by Jesus Christ, and God the Father, who raised him from the dead;) 2 And all the brethren which are with me, unto the churches of Galatia:

Notice that Paul uses the plural word *churches.* There were three churches located in the region of Galatia. It is located in Asia Minor in present-day Turkey. When we look at a map today, we see a land mass beneath the Black Sea and bordering the Mediterranean Sea. Within this area, referred to as Galatia, there were three cities in which Paul established churches:

Lystra, Derbe, and Lycaonia.

The cause of their present problem is explained in Acts 14:1-7:

> 1 **And it came to pass in Iconium, that they went both together into the synagogue of the Jews, and so spake, that a great multitude both of the Jews and also of the Greeks believed.**
>
> 2 **But the unbelieving Jews stirred up the Gentiles, and made their minds evil affected against the brethren.** 3 **Long time therefore abode they speaking boldly in the Lord, which gave testimony unto the word of his grace, and granted signs and wonders to be done by their hands.**
>
> 4 **But the multitude of the city was divided: and part held with the Jews, and part with the apostles.** 5 **And when there was an assault made both of**

[by] the Gentiles, and also of [by] the Jews with their rulers, to use them despitefully, and to stone them,

6 They were [a]ware of it, and fled unto Lystra and Derbe, cities of Lycaonia, and unto the region that lieth round about: 7 And there they preached the gospel.

We can see that a pattern is starting to form. Notice that the multitude of the city was divided between those who held to Paul's teaching and those that did not. Those that held to the Apostle Paul's teaching fled to Lystra, Derbe, and Lycaonia. It is to these three churches, collectively referred to as Galatia, that Paul now writes.

With this information, let us continue with our text. Galatians 1:3-5:

3 Grace be to you and peace from God the Father, and from our Lord Jesus Christ,

4 Who gave himself for our

**sins, that he might deliver us
from this present evil world,
according to the will of God
and our Father:**

**5 To whom be glory for ever
and ever. Amen.**

The assemblies in Galatia started out believing
the correct gospel, but the Judaizers came in
and started causing confusion by adding
things to Paul's gospel message. Verses 6-7:

**6 I marvel that ye are so soon re-
moved from him that called
you into the grace of Christ
unto another gospel:**

**7 Which is not another [gospel];
but there be some that trouble
you, and would pervert the
gospel of Christ.**

This perversion to Paul's gospel is not
another gospel at all. We should note that he is
not speaking about the Gospel of the Kingdom
which the Twelve were commissioned to
preach. Paul is writing about the one gospel
given to him by the Risen Lord for the Gentiles.

This is the only gospel that will save today in the Age of Grace. This Gospel of Grace is the one he had previously preached to the Galatian churches. We will see in a moment, it was subsequently altered into something else. The concept of changing the Gospel of Grace goes right to the heart of Galatians. It is its main theme.

Who was it that caused this change? They are referred to as *Judaizers*. These were Jews who came into the Body of Christ and convinced some of the people that they had to also observe the Law of Moses in order to be saved. Nowhere does Paul say that we must believe in Christ's finished work on the Cross *plus* keep the Law. The Gospel of Grace without works is a gospel of good news. The Gospel of Grace plus keeping the Law is not a gospel and it is not good news. It is for that reason Paul says he marvels that they are "so soon removed from him that called you into the grace of Christ unto another gospel" (v.6). This other gospel is not a legitimate gospel at all. It is a perversion of the gospel by mixing Law with Grace. We can do nothing to earn our salvation. We must just believe in the finished work in Christ's death, burial, and resurrection. Verses 8-9:

8 **But though we, or an angel from heaven, preach any other gospel unto you than that which we have preached unto you, let him be accursed.**

9 **As we said before, so say I now again, If any man preach any other gospel unto you than that ye have received, let him be accursed.**

The curse to which Paul refers is the *curse of the Law.* When perverting the Gospel of Grace by adding the Law, or works, they fall under the penalty of the Law. The penalty of the Law is death. See, we are not able to keep the Law. No one can. Furthermore, the Law cannot save us. Our observance of the Law cannot do anything for our salvation. In fact, works has nothing to do with salvation when we are saved by the Gospel of Grace. Paul makes this clear. Ephesians 2:8-9:

8 **<u>For by grace are ye saved through faith</u>; and that not of yourselves: it is the gift of God: 9 <u>Not of [by] works</u>, lest any man should boast.**

Paul specifically states that salvation is not by works. This prevents a man from boasting he had any part in his salvation. Works has nothing to do with grace. The book of Romans makes this clear. If we choose to put ourselves under the Law, then we put ourselves under the curse of the Law. The Law condemn us. It cannot save us. Romans 8:3-4:

3 For what the law could not do, in that it was weak through the flesh, God sending his own Son in the likeness of sinful flesh, and for sin, condemned sin in the flesh:

4 That the righteousness of the law might be fulfilled in us, who walk not after the flesh, but after the Spirit.

Because of the weakness of our flesh, righteousness by the Law cannot be attained. Again, it can only condemn us. To be righteous under the Law, we must be perfect. There is only One Who is perfect under the Law. This means keeping every point of the Law. If we fail to keep one point in the Law, we are guilty of it all. Christ fulfilled the Law for us. It is His righteousness that He makes available to those who choose, by faith, to believe.

Paul continues with this theme. Galatians 3:10-12:

> 10 **For as many as are of the works of the law are under the curse:** for it is written, **Cursed is every one that continueth not in all things which are written in the book of the law to do them.**

> 11 **But that** **no man is justified by the law in the sight of God,** **it is evident: for, The just shall live by faith.** 12 **And the law is not of faith:** **but, The man that doeth them shall live in them.**

Paul continues to make this point clear throughout Galatians. Think about this for a moment. How can we say that we have faith in what Christ has done while keeping the Law to earn our salvation? We just read that the Law is not by faith but by works. The man who keeps one foot on the land and one foot on a boat finds himself in a precarious position.

Either it is all about Christ's work and His grace towards us, or it is not. We cannot express our faith today by keeping the Law. In fact, by doing so, we do just the opposite. That is what the Galatians were starting to do when Paul wrote them.

We return to our text. Galatians 1:10-12:

10 For do I now persuade men, or God? or do I seek to please men? for if I yet pleased men, I should not be the servant of Christ.

11 But I certify you, brethren, that the gospel which was preached of me is not after man. 12 For I neither received it of [by] man, neither was I taught it, but by the revelation of Jesus Christ.

Paul's purpose was to persuade men about the truth he had received from the Resurrected Lord. He was not seeking to please men or obtain their approval. Rather he sought only the approval of the One Who appointed him as His messenger or apostle. At this point, Paul asserts that the message which he received was from the Resurrected Lord. He did not consort with the other Apostles who remained in Jerusalem after the resurrection. He was separated from them and received his own gospel.

We can confirm this. As the Apostles remained in Jerusalem, there arose suffering from the persecution that came after the resurrection. This is when Saul left for Damascus to persecute the Kingdom Believers. The entire story is laid out in Acts 9. On the road to Damascus, Paul had a personal encounter with his Savior. He was blinded and taken to Damascus. Acts 9:10-16:

> 10 **And there was a certain disciple at Damascus, named Ananias; and to him said the Lord in a vision, Ananias. And he said, Behold, I am here, Lord.**
>
> 11 **And the Lord said unto him, Arise, and go into the street which is called Straight, and enquire in the house of Judas for one called Saul, of Tarsus: for, behold, he prayeth,**

12 And hath seen in a vision a man named Ananias coming in, and putting his hand on him, that he might receive his sight.

13 Then Ananias answered, Lord, I have heard by many of [about] this man, how much evil he hath done to thy saints at Jerusalem: 14 And here he hath authority from the chief priests to bind all that call on thy name.

15 But the Lord said unto him, <u>Go thy way: for he is a chosen vessel unto me, to bear my name before the Gentiles, and kings, and the children of Israel</u>: 16 For I will shew him how great things he must suffer for my name's sake.

Paul received the message of the Gospel of Grace from the Lord Jesus Christ Himself. Galatians 1:13-14:

13 For ye have heard of my con-

versation [manner of living] in time past in the Jews' religion, how that beyond measure I persecuted the church of God, and wasted it:

14 And [I] profited in the Jews' religion above many my equals in mine own nation, being more exceedingly zealous of the traditions of my fathers.

Paul admits to persecuting Kingdom Believers. He was on the fast track for advancement within the Jewish religion. Yet, God had different plans for him. Paul confesses himself to be *the chief of sinners.* 1 Timothy 1:15:

15 This is a faithful saying, and worthy of all acceptation, that <u>Christ Jesus came into the world to save sinners; of whom I am chief</u>.

Paul says he was the worst of the worst because he persecuted the Kingdom Believers. Yet, God chose Paul for that very reason! God made Paul an example. Like a sewing pattern, a prototype is the first to be made of anything.

After that, its design is to be followed. Verse 16:

> 16 **Howbeit for this cause I ob-**
> **tained mercy, <u>that in me first</u>**
> **<u>Jesus Christ might shew forth</u>**
> **<u>all longsuffering, for a pattern</u>**
> **<u>to them which should hereaf-</u>**
> **<u>ter believe on him to life ever-</u>**
> **<u>lasting</u>.**

Did you notice that? Christ made Paul to be an example. Think about it. If Christ can save the worst of the worst by the Gospel of Grace, then He can save anyone! Paul would carry this message of salvation by grace through faith without works. He would preach the same gospel by which he himself was saved.

We return to our text. Galatians 1:15-17:

> 15 **But when it pleased God,**
> **who separated me from my**
> **mother's womb, and called me**
> **by his grace,**
>
> 16 **To reveal his Son in me, that**
> **I might preach him among the**
> **heathen; immediately I con-**
> **ferred not with flesh and**

blood:

17 Neither went I up to Jerusalem to them which were apostles before me; but I went into Arabia, and returned again unto Damascus.

Paul spoke with no man concerning his Gospel. Neither did he go to Jerusalem to confer with the other Apostles. He departed from Damascus and went to Arabia for three years. Where, it is believed, that the Lord tutored him face to face. Then, he returned to Damascus before ever going to Jerusalem. While in Jerusalem, he saw only Peter and James. Verses 18-20:

18 Then after three years I went up to Jerusalem to see Peter, and abode with him fifteen days. 19 But other of the apostles saw I none, save [except] James the Lord's brother.

20 Now the things which I write unto you, behold, before God, I lie not.

As the Apostle Paul continued his travels, he finds that he is known as the one who persecuted the Kingdom Believers. But now, he preaches the faith that he once sought to destroy. Verses 21-23:

> 21 **Afterwards I came into the regions of Syria and Cilicia;** 22 **And was unknown by face unto the churches of Judaea which were in Christ:**

> 23 **But they had heard only, That he which persecuted us in times past now preacheth the faith which once he destroyed.**

Only God has the power to save. Only He can do the impossible. He made the worst of the worst sinner into a "pattern" of His redeeming grace. Verse 24:

> 24 **And they glorified God in me.**

They saw what God had done in Paul and glorified God. Like the Apostle Paul, we too may glorify God because of what He has done in us.

2

Galatians 2 (Part I)

Paul makes a second journey to Jerusalem fourteen years after his first visit. Galatians 2:1:

> **1 Then fourteen years after I went up again to Jerusalem with Barnabas, and took Titus with me also.**

On this second trip, he was accompanied by Barnabas and Titus. We know that God revealed things to Paul, as His Apostle, that He did not reveal to anyone else. It was upon divine direction that Paul goes to Jerusalem, but he goes with a singular purpose. That purpose is to reveal to the other apostles what he had been directed to preach to the Gentiles. Verse 2:

2 And I went up by revelation, and communicated unto them that gospel which I preach among the Gentiles, but privately to them which were of reputation, lest by any means I should run, or had run, in vain.

Notice that Paul chose to speak to them privately. He wanted to avoid any potential conflict while accomplishing his purpose of informing the other apostles. In the previous chapter, we explained that grace and Law do not mix. Whereas the Law is bondage, grace is liberty. We will see this again. Verses 3-5:

3 But neither Titus, who was with me, being a Greek, was compelled to be circumcised:

4 And that because of false brethren unawares brought in, who came in privily to spy out our liberty which we have in Christ Jesus, that they might bring us into bondage:

5 To whom we gave place by subjection, no, not for an hour;

that the truth of the gospel might continue with you.

There were false brethren who had infiltrated the group. They were there to advocate for the Law and spy out the liberty under Paul's gospel. However, Paul and his crew held their ground in order that the Gospel of Grace might stand.

This was only the second meeting with Paul and the other apostles. In the other meeting, he had met only Peter and James. It is apparent that he was not familiar with the others. Verse 6:

> 6 **But of these who seemed to be somewhat, (whatsoever they were, it maketh no matter to me: God accepteth no man's person:) for they who seemed to be somewhat in conference added nothing to me:**

The others who were there and unknown to Paul talked amongst themselves, but in doing so, were unable to add anything to what Paul stated. In the following verses it becomes evident there is a dichotomy of messages here.

19

There are two different gospels. The group agrees that this is of God's doing and each group agrees to take their message to their respective recipients. Verses 7-8:

> 7 But contrariwise, when they saw that <u>the gospel of the un-circumcision</u> was committed unto me, as <u>the gospel of the circumcision</u> was unto Peter;

> 8 (For he that wrought effectually in Peter to the apostleship of the circumcision, the same was mighty in me toward the Gentiles:)

Even though it was explained earlier, it bears repeating. The Jews were God's people by covenant and they were physically marked by a covenantal requirement. They were to be circumcised. Therefore, the others, whether called Gentiles, heathen, or uncircumcised were not included in that covenant agreement nor subject to its requirement. It is from this distinction that the words in verse 8 take their meaning.

At this meeting, we see that another apostle has been added by name: Peter, James, . . . and John. Together, they agree to take their respective gospel messages to the ones God directed them. Verse 9:

> 9 **And when James, Cephas, and John, who seemed to be pillars, perceived the grace that was given unto me, they gave to me and Barnabas the right hands of fellowship; that <u>we should go unto the heathen [Gentiles]</u>, and <u>they unto the circumcision [Jews]</u>.**

This agreement also came with a special request. The saints who believed under the Gospel of the Kingdom were suffering greatly under persecution from the Romans, but also from the religious Jews who had rejected Christ as their Messiah. We can tell from Paul's response that he was more than willing to meet the other apostles' request. They asked for financial assistance for the beleaguered Kingdom Believers in Jerusalem. Verse 10:

> 10 **Only they would that we should remember the poor; the same which I also was forward**

to do.

Later, we find that the grace assemblies formed under the ministry of Paul were glad to provide assistance to the poor saints in Jerusalem. In addition to their persecution, we find another possible cause. In Acts 2, we find that all of them sold their possessions and had all things in common while they waited for the imminent arrival of the Kingdom. The Prophetic Program did not continue because God interrupted that Program to bring in the Dispensation of Grace. The Kingdom saints were left destitute and struggling. God used the charity of the Grace Believers to provide financial and material aid to the Kingdom Believers in need. Romans 15:25-27:

> 25 **But now I go unto Jerusalem to minister unto the saints.** 26 **For it hath pleased them of Macedonia and Achaia to make a certain contribution for the poor saints which are at Jerusalem.**
>
> 27 **It hath pleased them verily; and their debtors they are. For if the Gentiles have been made**

partakers of their spiritual things, their duty is also to minister unto them in carnal things.

Since Grace Believers also benefited from the Cross, it was only right that they should assist the poor Kingdom Believers in Jerusalem.

In verse 9, when we read that they "perceived the grace that was given" unto Paul, what does that mean? I believe that is referring to what Paul later explains in Ephesians 3:1-7:

> **1 For this cause I Paul, the prisoner of Jesus Christ for you Gentiles, 2 If ye have heard of <u>the dispensation of the grace of God which is given me</u> to you-ward:**
>
> **3 How that <u>by revelation he made known unto me the mystery;</u> (as I wrote afore in few words, 4 Whereby, when ye read, [that] <u>ye may understand my knowledge in the mystery of Christ)</u>**

5 Which in other ages was not made known unto the sons of men, as it is now revealed unto his holy apostles and prophets by the Spirit;

6 That the Gentiles should be fellowheirs, and of the same body, and partakers of his promise in Christ by the gospel:

7 Whereof I was made a minister, according to the gift of the grace of God given unto me by the effectual working of his power.

How did the Spirit make it known? It was revealed through the words which Paul preached.

Notice that the Gentiles also became *fellow-heirs* and *partakers of God's promise in Christ.* How did this happen? It was by the Gospel of Grace which Paul preached. He was made a minister according to the message of the Grace of God which he was given. There is that phrase again. God gave certain grace to Paul. It was this grace that first saved Paul in Acts 9. He was persecuting the Kingdom believers. He was the first sinner saved by grace. It was to Him that Christ entrusted the message of the dispensation of the Grace of God to be delivered to the Gentiles. Verse 8:

> 8 **<u>Unto me, who am less than the least of all saints, is this grace given</u>, that I should preach among the Gentiles the unsearchable riches of Christ;**

We cannot find this concept anywhere in the Old Testament regardless of how hard we search. This cannot be found in the four Gospels either. We can only find this in the revelation given to Paul by the Risen Lord.

There is an acknowledgement among them along with their apostolic blessings given to Paul by the Kingdom apostles. They give Paul and Barnabas the right hand of fellowship with the agreement made between these apostles. Each party had received specific authority from the Lord Jesus Christ to act as apostles. In this meeting, that fact is acknowledged.

How does that work exactly? What are

the mechanics involved? Let us think about this. The Dispensation of Grace has started and the message of salvation is by grace through faith in the finished work of the Cross. What, then, are Peter, James, John, and the other Apostles going to preach now? To answer this question, let us look at Galatians 6:15-16:

> 15 **For in Christ Jesus neither circumcision availeth any thing, nor uncircumcision, but a new creature. 16 And as many as walk according to this rule, peace be on them, and mercy, and upon the Israel of God.**

There is the physical nation called Israel and there is "the Israel of God." The latter is true or believing Israel. What does that mean? Romans 2:28-29:

> 28 **<u>For he is not a Jew, which is one outwardly;</u> neither is that circumcision, which is outward in the flesh:**
>
> 29 **<u>But he is a Jew, which is one inwardly;</u> and circumcision is that of the heart, in the spirit,**

and not in the letter; whose praise is not of men, but of God.

The point that Paul makes is anyone can be a physical descendent of Abraham, part of the twelve tribes of Israel. Any can be physically circumcised. However, a true Jew is one circumcised in the heart — spiritually part of true Israel, the Israel of God.

Before being stoned to death for preaching the Kingdom Gospel, Stephen stood before the Sanhedrin and addressed the religious leaders of Israel. Acts 7:51-53:

51 Ye stiffnecked and uncircumcised in heart and ears, ye do always resist the Holy Ghost: as your fathers did, so do ye.

52 Which of the prophets have not your fathers persecuted? and they have slain them which shewed before of the coming of the Just One; of whom ye have been now the betrayers and murderers:

53 [You] Who have received the law by the disposition of angels, and have not kept it.

He addressed the most pious of Israel's leadership. Notice his indictment is not only on them, but also on their ancestors. Again, here is the point. There are those who are the "physical circumcision" which is all of Israel. Then, there are those who are the "spiritual circumcision" which is "the Israel of God."

Peter, James, and John agreed to go to the circumcision which are the lost sheep of the house of Israel. They would remain in Jerusalem because of the persecution. The Prophetic Program would be temporarily suspended. However, the Gospel of the Kingdom will be preached in the future once the Age of Law, the Prophetic Program, resumes. In the meantime, God chose the Apostle Paul to go to all the world with the message of the Gospel of the Grace of God.

If this is true, then what are Peter, James, and the others to do? They are to continue to minister to the Kingdom Believers as they await the Kingdom. They still needed leadership. They still needed to understand what was going to happen. Therefore, Peter and the other apostles would minister to these Kingdom saints — true Israel. The books which follow Paul's letters (Hebrews to Revelation) were written to Kingdom Believers. They will instruct and comfort them during the coming Tribulation.

Here is an example of this. 2 Peter 3:1-2:

1 This second epistle, beloved, I now write unto you; in both which I stir up your pure minds by way of remembrance:

2 That ye may be mindful of the words which were spoken before by the holy prophets, and of the commandment of us the apostles of the Lord and Saviour:

Peter instructs his readers to remember what was taught to them by the prophets, the Law, and the Messiah. Verses 3-7:

3 Knowing this first, that there shall come in the last days

scoffers, walking after their own lusts, 4 And saying, Where is the promise of his coming? for since the fathers fell asleep, all things continue as they were from the beginning of the creation.

5 For this they willingly are ignorant of, that by the word of God the heavens were of old, and the earth standing out of the water and in the water: 6 Whereby the world that then was, being overflowed with water, perished:

7 But the heavens and the earth, which are now, by the same word are kept in store, reserved unto fire against the day of judgment and perdition of ungodly men.

Peter assures them that everything God said will happen, will happen! God will keep His promises. I think there are more important points to be made. Speaking to Kingdom Believers, we continue with verses 8-10:

8 But, beloved, be not ignorant of this one thing, that one day is with the Lord as a thousand years, and a thousand years as one day.

9 The Lord is not slack [remiss] concerning his promise, as some men count slackness; but is longsuffering to us-ward, not willing that any should perish, but that all should come to repentance.

10 But the day of the Lord will come as a thief in the night; in the which the heavens shall pass away with a great noise, and the elements shall melt with fervent heat, the earth also and the works that are therein shall be burned up.

For the Jews, nothing has changed. The "day of the Lord" refers to Jesus' return and pending judgment. It will be like "a thief in the night." Again, nothing with God changed and the following confirms it. Verses 11-13:

11 Seeing then that all these things shall be dissolved, what manner of persons ought ye to be in all holy conversation [manner of living] and godliness,

12 Looking for and hasting unto the coming of the day of God, wherein the heavens being on fire shall be dissolved, and the elements shall melt with fervent heat?

13 Nevertheless we, according to his promise, look for new heavens and a new earth, wherein dwelleth righteousness.

All this is part of the Prophetic Program as recorded by the Old Testament prophets. Verse 14:

14 Wherefore, beloved, seeing that ye look for such things, be diligent that ye may be found of him in peace, without spot, and blameless.

In his epistles, Peter writes to true Israel, those who follow the Gospel of the Kingdom. He tells them that everything the prophets foretold will still come true. However, there was a delay in the Prophetic Program. We will continue with this in the next chapter.

3

Galatians 2 (Part II)

Continuing from the previous chapter, Peter makes a reference to the Apostle Paul. 2 Peter 3:15-16:

> **15 And account that the long-suffering of our Lord is salvation; even as our beloved brother Paul also according to the wisdom given unto him hath written unto you;**

> **16 As also in all his epistles, speaking in them of these things; in which are some things hard to be understood, which they that are unlearned and unstable wrest [twist], as they do also the other scrip-**

**tures, unto their own destruc-
tion.**

In other words, the fact that Christ has not yet come back in judgment means salvation by grace is available to both individual Gentiles and individual Jews. It gives everyone an opportunity for salvation in the Age of Grace.

Many people use verse 15 to support the idea that Paul wrote Hebrews to the same recipients of Peter's letters. The Hebrews epistle was unsigned by its author and, perhaps, that is for good reason. Referring to Paul's epistles collectively, Peter acknowledges that some things contained therein are hard to understand. This is a wonderful endorsement of credibility coming from Peter. He goes on to say that many people try to twist Paul's writings as they do so with *other scripture* at their own peril. Peter finishes his thought with verse 17:

> 17 **Ye therefore, beloved, seeing ye know these things before, beware lest ye also, being led away with the error of the wicked, fall from your own stedfastness.**

He encourages them to remain steadfast. In other words, Peter tells them to hold their ground. He assures them the Prophetic Program is going to be fulfilled. Furthermore, if they want to understand why it is delayed, they are going to have to read what Paul wrote. They will understand why the Tribulation has not come and why Christ has not yet set up his Kingdom on earth. All of this, they can understand from Paul's writings.

Peter and the other apostles continued to minister to the circumcision — believing Israel — who were waiting for the arrival of the Kingdom. He encouraged them to keep on the right path while waiting for the fulfillment of God's promises. That is my explanation as to why Peter remained in Jerusalem with the other apostles. They continued ministering to the circumcision. However, with the appearance of Paul, they were no longer continuing to preach the Gospel of the Kingdom to unbelieving Jews. They now understood why the Prophetic Program was on hold.

By agreement, Paul and Barnabas would go "unto the heathen." Previously, we had explained that *heathen* is another word for non-

Jews. They were the followers of false gods and not members of the commonwealth of Israel. Other words by which they may be called include: gentiles, nations, pagans, and the uncircumcised. Here is a question. Could that also include unbelieving Jews? There are two verses I would like us to consider. The Lord had just appeared to Saul of Tarsus and saved him. The Lord is responding to Ananias' hesitation to go and heal Paul's blindness. Acts 9:15:

> 15 **But the Lord said unto him, Go thy way: for he is a chosen vessel unto me, <u>to bear my name before the Gentiles, and kings, and the children of Israel</u>:**

After Paul's healing, he began his ministry, but to whom did he minister? Verse 17-19:

> 17 **And Ananias went his way, and entered into the house; and putting his hands on him said, Brother Saul, the Lord, even Jesus, that appeared unto thee in the way as thou camest, hath sent me, that thou might-**

est receive thy sight, and be filled with the Holy Ghost.

18 And immediately there fell from his eyes as it had been scales: and he received sight forthwith, and arose, and was baptized.

19 And when he had received meat, he was strengthened. Then was Saul certain days with the disciples which were at Damascus.

We find our answer in verses 20-22:

20 And straightway he preached Christ in the synagogues, that he is the Son of God.

21 But all that heard him were amazed, and said; Is not this he that destroyed them which called on this name in Jerusalem, and came hither for that intent, that he might bring them bound unto the chief

priests?

22 But Saul increased the more in strength, and confounded the Jews which dwelt at Damascus, proving that this is very [truly] Christ.

To whom did Paul first preach Christ? He preached in the synagogues that Christ is the Son of God. Where did Paul go? He went into the synagogues. He went to the Jews first. Acts 14:1:

1 And it came to pass in Iconium, that they went both together into the synagogue of the Jews . . .

This applies to Paul and Barnabas who arrived at Iconium. Here is the remainder of verse 1:

1 . . . and so spake, that a great multitude both of the Jews and also of the Greeks believed.

This continues throughout the initial part of Paul's ministry. He goes to the Jew first; then to the Gentiles. When he came to a town, he

First would go to the synagogue. Acts 17:1-4:

1 Now when they had passed through Amphipolis and Apollonia, they came to Thessalonica, where was a synagogue of the Jews:

2 And Paul, as his manner was, went in unto them, and three sabbath days reasoned with them out of the scriptures,

3 Opening and alleging, that Christ must needs have suffered, and risen again from the dead; and that this Jesus, whom I preach unto you, is Christ [the Anointed One].

4 And some of them believed, and consorted with Paul and Silas; and of the devout Greeks a great multitude, and of the chief women not a few.

He makes his position clear in Romans 1:16:

16 For I am not ashamed of the

gospel of Christ: for <u>it is the</u> <u>power of God unto salvation to</u> <u>every one that believeth; to the</u> <u>Jew first, and also to the Greek</u>.

Paul considers unbelieving Jews in the same manner as he does the Gentiles because they both are outside of God's salvation plan. Paul compares the Gentiles to the Jews in this Age of Grace. Romans 3:9-12:

> **9 What then? are we better than they? No, in no wise [way]: for we have before proved both Jews and Gentiles, that they are all under sin;**
>
> **10 As it is written, There is none righteous, no, not one: 11 There is none that understandeth, there is none that seeketh after God.**
>
> **12 They are all gone out of the way, they are together become unprofitable; there is none that doeth good, no, not one.**

For Paul, there was no different between the

unbelieving Jew and the unbelieving Gentile.

Now, the Kingdom Believers wait for their promises. Hebrews 11:13:

> **13 These all died in faith, not having received the promises, but having seen them afar off, and were persuaded of them, and embraced them, and confessed that they were strangers and pilgrims on the earth.**

Today, nearly 2000 years after the death and resurrection of Christ, believing Jews still wait in faith. Faith is believing regardless of how long someone must wait.

With this information, we can continue with Galatians 2:11:

> **11 But when Peter was come to Antioch, I withstood him to the face, because he was to be blamed**

We could call Antioch the headquarters for Paul's ministry. It is home for the first Grace Believers who accepted Paul's gospel message.

When Peter came to Antioch, Paul confronted him face to face for something Peter had done. Verses 12-13:

> 12 **For before that certain came from James, he did eat with the Gentiles: but when they were come, he withdrew and separated himself, fearing them which were of the circumcision.**

> 13 **And the other Jews dissembled likewise with him; insomuch that Barnabas also was carried away with their dissimulation.**

Peter ate and fellowshipped with the Gentiles until the others from Jerusalem arrived in Antioch. Once they arrived, Peter distanced himself from the Gentile believers and fellowshipped only with the Jews. To make matters worse, Barnabas also joined Peter. Many of whom were the religious Jews from Jerusalem who followed the Law. They believed that it was wrong to break bread with Gentiles. The word "dissemble" means "the inclination or practice of misleading others through lies or trickery." Similarly, what a wolf would do to lead sheep astray. The word "dissimulation" is comparable to "artifice, cheating, craftiness, crookedness, deceitfulness, deception, dishonesty, fraud, and wiliness." Bottomline, Paul saw Peter as a hypocrite and the negative effect he had on Barnabas with his pious behavior.

Paul confronted Peter publicly. Verse 14:

14 But when I saw that they walked not uprightly according to the truth of the gospel, I said unto Peter before them all, If thou, being a Jew, livest after the manner of Gentiles, and not as do the Jews, why compellest thou the Gentiles to live as do the Jews?

He accused Peter of being a hypocrite. Fellowshipping with the Gentiles, but, when the Jews came, he would have nothing to do with them. It was hypocrisy. Why? Perhaps, Peter was trying to appease the Jews. Verse 15:

15 We who are Jews by nature, and not sinners of the Gentiles,

In other words, they are Jews by nature. They are the physical seed of Abraham. They have been circumcised. They know the Law. Have you ever been to a church where there is a division like this? There are the sinners saved by grace. Then, there are the righteous ones who are above reproach. They are not *sinners* like the others.

Paul gives a response. Verse 16:

16 Knowing that a man is not justified by the works of the law, but by the faith of Jesus Christ, even we have believed in Jesus Christ, that we might be justified by the faith of Christ, and not by the works of the law: for by the works of the law shall no flesh be justified.

Here is an important point. Justification comes by faith. The act of keeping the Law never saved anyone. However, believing what God said, that is the faith that justifies. No one can please God without faith. Paul adds to this point: if we are saved, we are saved by Jesus Christ. It is His finished work; not ours.

This applies to the Kingdom Believers as well. However, they are required to maintain their faith and provide evidence of their faith by good works. (See James 2:14-17.) Forgiveness of their sins comes at their Messiah's return. (See Matthew 24:13.)

Let us continue. Verses 17-18.

17 But if, while we seek to be justified by Christ, we ourselves also are found sinners, is therefore Christ the minister of sin? God forbid.

18 For if I build again the things which I destroyed, I make myself a transgressor.

Paul is saying that if they put themselves back under the Law, it makes them transgressors and the Law will condemn them. If the Law says, "thou shalt not" and they do anyways, then they are guilty under the Law. Therefore, they are condemned. There are over 600 points to the Law. Each and every point must be obeyed. The Apostle James writes to the Kingdom Believers. He states that if they are guilty in one point, they are guilty of the whole thing.

Therefore, the Law can only condemn.

It is Christ's finished work on the Cross that takes care of those saved by the Gospel of the Grace of God. Colossians 2:13-15:

> 13 **And you, being dead in your sins and the uncircumcision of your flesh, hath he quickened together with him, having forgiven you all trespasses;**
>
> 14 **Blotting out the handwriting of ordinances that was against us, which was contrary to us, and took it out of the way, nailing it to his cross;**
>
> 15 **And having spoiled principalities and powers, he made a shew of them openly, triumphing over them in it.**

The word "quickened" means "made alive." This is so incredible! How grateful we should be that all our trespasses have been forgiven, but there is more to it than that. The charges which were against us, referring to the Law, have been taken away. Christ nailed the Law to the Cross. The performance system we were under, the one that continually condemns us, was nailed to the Cross. He took their transgressions and blotted them out! If anyone who is saved by grace puts themself back under the Law, then what have they done? They have made themselves a transgressor.

I love these next two verses. They show us the difference between Christians who are trying to live their Christian life by the Law and Christians who are living their Christian life under grace. Galatians 2:19-20:

> 19 **For I through the law am dead to the law, that I might live unto God.**
>
> 20 **I am crucified with Christ: nevertheless I live; yet not I, but Christ liveth in me: and the life which I now live in the flesh I live by the faith of the Son of God, who loved me, and gave himself for me.**

That is the difference between someone living under the Law and someone living under Grace. The former is always making himself a transgressor by striving to keep the Law but failing. The latter says, "I'm dead to the Law and crucified with Christ and Christ lives in me." This is how we live for God. This is how we serve God. This is how we live our Christian life. The Law can do nothing for us. It can only condemn us.

The chapter closes with verse 21:

21 I do not frustrate the grace of God: for if righteousness come by the law, then Christ is dead in vain.

If the Law plays any part in our salvation, then Christ died for nothing. We really need to understand that Christ did it all. What glorious news for sinners! This should motivate us to live for Him because we are dead yet we live in Christ. He fulfilled the Law on our behalf. He has forgiven our sins—past, present, and future. Now, He lives in us!

4

Galatians 3 (Part I)

In this chapter, Paul continues his chastisement of the Galatian assemblies who have changed the gospel into something that is not a gospel. Galatians 3:1:

> **1 O foolish Galatians, who hath bewitched you, that ye should not obey the truth, before whose eyes Jesus Christ hath been evidently set forth, crucified among you?**

He refers to the time when he first came to them and preached the Gospel of Grace. At that time, they saw with eyes of faith. As Paul laid out the evidence of what Jesus had done for them, they understood, and it saved them. That change was visible in the assemblies of

Galatia. He writes and asks them "who hath bewitched you?" In this context, "bewitched" means "to be persuaded to believe a false doctrine through deceit."

He continues. Verse 2:

2 This only would I learn of you, <u>Received ye the Spirit by the works of the law, or by the hearing of faith?</u>

In Romans, Paul tells us that faith comes by hearing, and hearing by the Word of God (*cf.* Rom. 10:17). Paul reminds the Galatians that when he preached the Gospel of Grace to them initially, they believed. We understand that it is by hearing the preaching of the Gospel that we have faith to believe. That is how we receive the Spirit. Furthermore, we are sealed by that Spirit until the day of redemption. , something has changed. Verse 3:

3 Are ye so foolish? having begun in the Spirit, are ye now made perfect by the flesh?

What is Paul saying here? He is equating the works of Law as being made perfect by the flesh. Did you see that? In verse 2, he asked them a direct question, "Did they receive the Spirit by the works of the Law or by the hearing of faith?" Then, he continues to question them, "Have you become so foolish? Have you lost all reason?" He is asking whether they truly believed the Gospel of Grace since they are now striving to be made perfect by "the works of the Law."

The "works of the Law" is the requirement to keep the Law. This is an act of the flesh. It bases salvation upon the efforts of man and not upon the finished work of Christ. Whether it is to obtain salvation or to maintain salvation, it diminishes the work of Christ by adding human effort. That is what Paul is talking about when he refers to the flesh. His tone is accusatory. So, you foolish Galatians, you started out being saved by grace through faith, but now you believe you are saved because of something you do or don't do? Can you see how foolish this is? Paul refers to this as being "of the flesh" because it appeals to their pride or sin nature. It allows them to boast to others about what they have done or not done as a matter of pride. They can then compare themselves to others in the church to see who is a better or more pious member. All this plays to their egos or to their flesh. Paul wrote to the Grace Believers in Ephesus. Ephesians 2:8-9:

> 8 **For by grace are ye saved through faith; and that not of yourselves: it is the gift of God:**
>
> 9 **Not of [by] works, lest any man should boast.**

Notice his comment about boasting. That is how the sin nature works. It wants to boast that it is righteous on its own. Paul wants the Galatians to understand this.

He goes on. Galatians 3:4:

> 4 **Have ye suffered so many things in vain? if it be yet in vain.**

They suffered for being a believer and, having suffered so many things, they failed to yield the desired outcome. He is telling them that their suffering was fruitless unless it eventually proves to be fruitful. They still have time to fix this. Verse 5:

5 He therefore that ministereth to you the Spirit, and worketh miracles among you, doeth he it by the works of the law, or by the hearing of faith?

At this time, miracles, signs and wonders were still being manifested through the Holy Spirit. He asks them who ministered to them through the Spirit. It was Paul who ministered. Did he do it by works of the Law or by the preaching of the faith? Romans 10:17:

17 So then faith cometh by hearing, and hearing by the word of God.

God sent Paul to preach salvation by grace through faith. The Galatians heard the Word of God and believed. He makes his point by asking them whether it came by the Law or by faith. So, preaching to them and working miracles both come from the Spirit and not by the works of the Law. The Spirit of God will not work without faith. Galatians 3:6:

6 Even as Abraham believed God, and it was accounted to him for righteousness.

Paul quotes from Genesis 15:6:

> **6 And he [Abraham] believed in the LORD; and he [the LORD] counted it to him for righteousness.**

Why is Paul referring to Abraham? We find the answer in the following. Galatians 3:7:

> **7 Know ye therefore that <u>they which are of faith, the same are the children of Abraham</u>.**

Paul makes an important point. Just as Abraham believed what God told him and his faith was counted to him as righteousness, so too the Galatians must exercise their faith. They must believe the Gospel of Grace. This applies to us today. When we believe what God is telling us, what God has revealed to us through Paul, then we are, in a spiritual sense, the same as the children of Abraham. They must accept and believe God's Word. Abraham was the first man in the Bible to be justified by faith alone! By doing that, God credited righteousness to him. Therefore, Abraham is also referred to as "the father of faith." We are like him. We believe the message God sent to us through Paul. Believing Christ's finished work through His death, burial, and resurrection gives us the righteousness of Christ through faith. We share in Abraham's heritage of faith.

Although Paul refers to Grace Believers as "children" of Abraham's faith, we are not physically the children of Abraham. We will not inherit the physical blessings which God promised Abraham and his descendants. This is on a spiritual level because we too receive righteousness by faith. Paul continues. Verses 8-9:

> 8 And the scripture, foreseeing that God would justify the heathen [Gentiles] through faith, preached before the gospel unto Abraham, saying, In thee shall all nations be blessed.

> 9 So then they which be of faith are blessed with faithful Abraham.

Let us stop for a moment to think about this. We know that God is the Author of Scripture. We know He has infinite knowledge of the past, present, and future. So, there is no question that He knew in advance that in the future He would justify the heathen, the Gentiles, through faith. God knew this when He told the good news to Abraham concerning all the nations being blessed through him. For this reason, we are blessed along with faithful Abraham.

Here is the point. We are not the physical seed of Abraham. However, there is one Seed that came from Abraham. That Seed is the Lord Jesus Christ. He is a direct descendant of Abraham. (See Matthew 1:1; Luke 3:34.) Jesus Christ is the singular Seed to which God was referring when He spoke the promise that through Abraham would all the nations, the Gentiles, be blessed. Abraham knew nothing about the Gospel of the Grace of God. That was kept a mystery until it was revealed to Paul. However, that was *good news* to Abraham that through his Seed, the Lord Jesus Christ, all the nations of the earth will be blessed. Spiritually, we share in Abraham's heritage of faith and, as a result, we share in his spiritual blessing of righteousness by faith. Verse 10:

10 For as many as are of the works of the law are under the curse: for it is written, Cursed is every one that continueth not in all things which are written in the book of the law to do them.

Paul referred to the same thing at the opening of Galatians. (Gal. 1:8.) In that verse, those who altered the Gospel of Grace preached by Paul would be "accursed." Salvation by grace cannot be mixed with keeping the commandments or doing good works. If we do, then it is no longer salvation by the gift of grace but rather by our own merit. Verses 11-12:

11 But that no man is justified by the law in the sight of God, it is evident: for, The just shall live by faith.

12 And the law is not of faith: but, The man that doeth them shall live in them.

Faith applies to every dispensation and not the Dispensation of Grace alone. Everyone who wanted to be in a right position with God had to have faith. Concerning the Jews, they too must live by faith. The following verse applies to the Jews after the Rapture. Hebrews 11:6:

> 6 But without faith it is impossible to please him: for he that cometh to God must believe that he is, and that he is a rewarder of them that diligently seek him.

The Jews are required to do good works as evidence of their faith, but it is never works that saves them. Their faith saves them. Galatians 3:13:

> 13 Christ hath redeemed us from the curse of the law, being made a curse for us: for it is written, Cursed is every one that hangeth on a tree:

The above comes from the Old Testament. Deuteronomy 21:22-23:

> 22 And <u>if a man have committed a sin worthy of death, and</u>

he be to be put to death, and thou hang him on a tree:

23 His body shall not remain all night upon the tree, but thou shalt in any wise bury him that day; (for he that is hanged is accursed of God;) that thy land be not defiled, which the LORD thy God giveth thee for an inheritance.

Paul refers to what Jesus Christ did for us. He took our place when He became sin for us. The purpose of hanging someone on a tree was so that others would know that they committed sin worthy of death. Christ took upon Himself all of our sin and was punished on the Cross — the tree — for our accursed sins.

Why did Jesus Christ hang on that tree for us? Why did He become the curse for us? We must always read the whole text to fully understand it. Galatians 3:14:

14 That the blessing of Abraham might come on the Gentiles through Jesus Christ; that we might receive the promise

of the Spirit through faith.

The blessing of Abraham, to which Paul refers, was God's imputed righteousness to Abraham for his faith. Like Abraham, when we believe what God said, we too have the same blessing of Abraham. Therefore, when we believe the Gospel of Grace, Christ imputes His righteousness to us. When we put our faith in Christ's death, burial, and resurrection, our sin and its penalty becomes paid in full. His righteousness is then imputed to us. That is the blessing of Abraham.

Upon salvation, we "receive the promise of the Spirit through faith." Consider what Paul wrote. Ephesians 1:13-14:

> 13 **In whom ye also trusted, <u>after that ye heard the word of truth, the gospel of your salvation: in whom also after that ye believed, ye were sealed with that holy Spirit of promise,</u>**
>
> 14 **Which is <u>the earnest of our inheritance until the redemption of the purchased possession,</u> unto the praise of his glo-**

ry.

The word *earnest* is a legal term. It is used in legal agreements to mean "a deposit to secure the completion of a transaction agreed to by two or more parties." Think about it. The "holy Spirit of promise secures the completion of a transaction. What transaction is that? We were bought by the blood of Christ. We belong to Him. It is the "holy Spirit of promise" Who secures the completion of "the redemption of the purchase position."

In the next chapter, we will continue with this matter and find out more about this covenant God made with Abraham.

5

Galatians 3 (Part II)

In the previous chapter, we ended with a quote from Ephesians 1:13-14:

> 13 **In whom ye also trusted, after that ye heard the word of truth, the gospel of your salvation: in whom also after that ye believed, ye were sealed with that holy Spirit of promise,**
>
> 14 **Which is <u>the earnest of our inheritance until the redemption of the purchased possession</u>, unto the praise of his glory.**

This has to do with the inheritance of Grace Believers. It speaks about "the redemption of the purchased possession." It refers to our physical redemption (Rapture) as our salvation was purchased by the blood of Christ.

Paul connects this with the covenant God made with Abraham. Galatians 3:15:

> **15 Brethren, I speak after the manner of men; Though it be but a man's covenant, yet if it be confirmed, no man disannulleth, or addeth thereto.**

A covenant is a legally binding document between two or more parties. Once it has been confirmed, nobody can nullify or change this legally binding agreement. What Paul is saying that that the covenant that God made with Abraham is legally binding. It cannot be nullified. It cannot be changed in any way. Verse 16:

> **16 <u>Now to Abraham and his seed were the promises made.</u> He saith not, And to seeds, as of many; but as of one, <u>And to thy seed, which is Christ.</u>**

The word "seed" can mean one seed or it can mean many. Paul makes it clear the intended use is singular. This is a new revelation from God to us. Let us return to Genesis and look again at the promises God made to Abraham. Genesis 12:1-3:

> 1 **Now the LORD had said unto Abram, Get thee out of thy country, and from thy kindred, and from thy father's house, unto a land that I will shew thee:**
>
> 2 **And I will make of thee a great nation, and I will bless thee, and make thy name great; and thou shalt be a blessing:** 3 **And I will bless them that bless thee, and curse him that curseth thee: and <u>in thee shall all families of the earth be blessed.</u>**

Let us go to Genesis 17:1-7:

> 1 **And when Abram was ninety years old and nine, the LORD appeared to Abram, and said unto him, I am the Almighty God; walk before me, and be**

thou perfect.

2 And I will make my covenant between me and thee, and will multiply thee exceedingly. 3 And Abram fell on his face: and God talked with him, saying,

4 As for me, behold, my covenant is with thee, and thou shalt be a father of many nations. 5 Neither shall thy name any more be called Abram, but thy name shall be Abraham; for a father of many nations have I made thee.

6 And I will make thee exceeding fruitful, and I will make nations of thee, and kings shall come out of thee. 7 And I will establish my covenant between me and thee and thy seed after thee in their generations for an everlasting covenant, to be a God unto thee, and to thy seed after thee.

This is an everlasting covenant. There can be no changes or additions. Abraham did not know any more than God told him. He did not know that the one Seed would be the Lord Jesus Christ. There are three parties to this covenant: God, Abraham, and the Lord Jesus Christ—the Promised Messiah. Abraham and his children after him all assumed that the covenant was with Abraham and all his descendants. However, it is through this singular Seed that Israel and all the other nations are blessed. This revelation was given to the Apostle Paul.

Remember, the prophetic promises do not apply to the Body of Christ. After the Rapture, these other nations who blessed Israel during the Tribulation, will be blessed through Israel (See Genesis 12:3.) At that point, Israel will be a nation of priests serving Christ the King in Jerusalem. (See 1 Peter 2:9-10.) It is important that we see that what is going on today is different. Romans 11:7-12:

> 7 What then? Israel hath not obtained that which he seeketh for; but the election hath obtained it, and the rest were blinded 8 (According as it is written, God hath given them

the spirit of slumber, eyes that they should not see, and ears that they should not hear;) unto this day.

9 And David saith, Let their table be made a snare, and a trap, and a stumblingblock, and a recompence unto them: 10 Let their eyes be darkened, that they may not see, and bow down their back alway.

11 I say then, Have they stumbled that they should fall? God forbid: but rather through their fall salvation is come unto the Gentiles, for to provoke them to jealousy.

12 Now if the fall of them be the riches of the world, and the diminishing of them the riches of the Gentiles; how much more their fulness?

It is through the fall of Israel that Gentiles have this opportunity for the blessing of the Spirit through faith. Romans 11:25-27:

25 For I would not, brethren, that ye should be ignorant of this mystery, lest ye should be wise in your own conceits; that blindness in part is happened to Israel, until the fulness of the Gentiles be come in.

26 And so all Israel shall be saved: as it is written, There shall come out of Sion the Deliverer, and shall turn away ungodliness from Jacob:

27 For this is my covenant unto them, when I shall take away their sins.

This was a mystery that Israel would fall and, through their fall, the Gentiles would have the opportunity to be saved by grace through faith. This period of time, called the Age of Grace, lasts for only a while. It will end abruptly at the Rapture and, at that point, God will fulfill the covenants and promises He made with Israel.

At His Second Coming, He will remove Israel's sins and establish His eternal Kingdom. Let us finish with verses 28-32:

28 As concerning the gospel, they are enemies for your sakes: but as touching the election, they are beloved for the fathers' sakes. 29 For the gifts and calling of God are without repentance.

30 For as ye in times past have not believed God, yet have now obtained mercy through their unbelief:

31 Even so have these also now not believed, that through your mercy they also may obtain mercy.

32 For God hath concluded them all in unbelief, that he might have mercy upon all.

This mystery concerned the fall of Israel, but as we know, their fall is only temporary. God will fulfill the promises He made to them. Galatians 3:16-18:

16 Now to Abraham and his seed were the promises made.

He saith not, And to seeds, as of many; but as of one, And to thy seed, which is Christ.

17 And this I say, that the covenant, that was confirmed before of God in Christ, the law, which was four hundred and thirty years after, cannot disannul, that it should make the promise of none effect.

18 <u>For if the inheritance be of the law, it is no more of promise: but God gave it to Abraham by promise.</u>

Grace Believers receive salvation by grace through faith. They immediately receive "the holy Spirit of Promise" as earnest or guaranty. That is how individual Gentiles and individual Jews can be saved today. This is the result of Abraham's Seed (singular) Who is the Christ. He is Abraham's descendent. This can be verified by the genealogy of Jesus Christ beginning in Matthew 1:1:

1 <u>The book of the generation of Jesus Christ, the son of David,</u>

the son of Abraham.

Both the blessings and promises that God made to Abraham and David come through Jesus Christ Who is their Seed.

God's promise of righteousness through faith came from the Abrahamic Covenant. God made the Mosaic Covenant, containing the Law, 430 years later. Therefore, "For if the inheritance be of the law, it is no more of promise: but God gave it to Abraham by promise" (v. 18). The point that Paul makes here is this: the covenant God made with Abraham cannot be voided by the Law. The penalties for failure to keep the Law cannot make the promises of the Abrahamic Covenant useless or void. The Law cannot alter or supersede God's promises to Abraham!

In the next chapter, we will finish Galatians 3 and consider the purpose or usefulness of the Law.

6

Galatians 3 (Part III)

Paul focuses on the purpose of the Law. He asks the Galatians one question. Why are you serving the Law? You have the blessing of Abraham which is righteousness through faith. The Law has no relevance to the blessings that you already have. You also have the gracious promise of salvation through faith alone without the Law. So, again, why do you still serve the Law? Galatians 3:19:

> 19 **Wherefore then serveth the law? It was added because of transgressions, till the seed [Jesus Christ] should come to whom the promise was made; and it was ordained by angels in the hand of a mediator.**

God gave the Law to Israel because of their transgressions. He wanted to show Israel that they were sinners and could not do it themselves. They needed a Savior! They are unable to keep the Law. They are sinners and need a Savior just like everyone else. God deals with men in different ways at different times. God dealt with Abraham one way because of his faith. He dealt with Israel another way because of their lack of faith. He placed them under the Law to teach them. Verse 20:

20 **Now a mediator is not a mediator of one, but God is one.**

The word "mediator" means "someone who intercedes between two parties, who can act indifferently between contending parties with a view toward reconciliation." In different dispensations, God mediates with men in different ways, yet He is One. Verse 21-22:

21 **Is the law then against the promises of God? God forbid: for if there had been a law given which could have given life, verily righteousness should have been by the law.**

22 But <u>the scripture hath con-cluded all under sin, that the promise by faith of Jesus Christ might be given to them that believe</u>.

Paul writes that Scripture has condemned all under sin for a reason. It is so that the promise of salvation by the faithfulness of Jesus Christ can be given to all who believe. Romans 4:3-5:

3 For what saith the scripture? Abraham believed God, and it was counted unto him for righteousness.

4 Now <u>to him that worketh is the reward not reckoned of grace, but of debt</u>. **5** But <u>to him that worketh not, but believeth on him that justifieth the un-godly, his faith [like Abra-ham's] is counted for right-eousness</u>.

Abraham received righteousness because he believed God. He received it as a gift. If we work for salvation, then our salvation is not a gift of God. It is a debt that we feel God owes us. If we do not work to earn our salvation, but instead trust in His Word, then our salvation is based upon our faith in what God has said.

Let us return to Galatians 3:23:

23 But before faith came, we were kept under the law, shut up unto the faith which should afterwards be revealed.

This is a dispensational point. In the past, there was no salvation for Gentiles outside of Israel. Ephesians 2:11-13:

11 Wherefore remember, that ye being in time past Gentiles in the flesh, who are called Un-circumcision by that which is called the Circumcision in the flesh made by hands;

12 That at that time ye were without Christ, being aliens from the commonwealth of Is-rael, and strangers from the covenants of promise, having no hope, and without God in the world:

13 But now in Christ Jesus ye who sometimes were far off are made nigh [near] by the blood of Christ.

It says, "before faith came." Faith was shut up or hidden until it should be revealed according to God's plan. That plan was salvation for the Gentiles through the Gospel of Grace.

For Bible students, here is a question: When did the Law stop being in effect? The Age of Law was temporarily suspended when the Dispensation of Grace started. We are operating under God's grace and mercy without judgment under the Law. Christ first revealed this glorious new dispensation to the Apostle Paul. This was the new message of salvation by grace through faith. Paul was the first to be saved by grace through faith. He was the pattern or prototype which all other Grace Believers should follow. Currently, the Law is of no effect. Therefore, the faith that Paul preaches could not have been known until the Law was suspended and the Dispensation of Grace began.

Let us move on. Galatians 3: 24-25:

24 Wherefore the law was our schoolmaster to bring us unto Christ, that we might be justified by faith.

25 But after that faith is come, we are no longer under a schoolmaster.

Paul makes the purpose of the Law clear. It was to show Israel that they were sinners and lead them to their Messiah. There was a lesson to be learned. It was intended to show Israel that they need their Messiah and Savior. The Law does what a schoolmaster does. As their schoolmaster, the Law was to teach Israel. They could not keep the Law on their own. Israel needed a Savior.

Now that salvation by faith has come, there is a choice to be made. Those who choose not to believe the Gospel of Grace will be judged by their own unrighteousness. The Law will lead to their condemnation and death. Those who do not trust in the finished work of Christ on the Cross and accept His righteousness, will have no defense at their judgment. Verse 26:

26 For ye are all the children of God by faith in Christ Jesus.

Our faith must be in the faithfulness of Christ. It is so important for us to understand this. It is the second time that Paul has made this point. Look back at Galatians 2:16:

16 Knowing that a man is not justified by the works of the law, but by the faith of Jesus Christ, even we have believed in Jesus Christ, that we might be justified by the faith of Christ, and not by the works of the law: for by the works of the law shall no flesh be justified.

Notice that Paul says, "the faith of Jesus Christ." This refers to *His faithfulness!* He was faithful to the Heavenly Father to complete the necessary work for our salvation. Therefore, we must believe in "the faith of Jesus Christ."

We return to Galatians 3: 27-28:

27 For as many of you as have been baptized into Christ have put on Christ.

28 There is neither Jew nor Greek [Gentile], there is neither bond nor free, there is neither male nor female: for ye are all one in Christ Jesus.

There is some controversy over these verses. So, let us take a moment and think about them. The phrase "baptized into Christ" has caused a problem for some. Is it not the Holy Spirit Who baptizes believers into Christ? The Spirit of God baptized us the moment we believed. We are spiritually baptized into Christ and, therefore being in Christ, we are a new creature. The old things have passed away and all things are new. It was not water baptism that put us into Christ. This important work is done by the Spirit; not by water. It is the operation of the Holy Spirit that puts us in Christ when we believe the Gospel. As the result of this baptism by the Holy Spirit, there is no distinction between Jew or Gentile, slave or free; male or female. It tells us that, concerning this spiritual baptism, all of us are one in Christ Jesus.

At the beginning of Galatians 3, we discussed that Christ is Abraham's Seed (singular). He is the One to fulfill the promise God made to Abraham. Paul made the point that we have "the faith of Christ." And, our trust is in "the faithfulness of Christ." Spiritually we are placed in Him. With these things in mind, Paul closes this chapter. Verse 29:

> **29 And if ye be Christ's, then are ye Abraham's seed, and heirs according to the promise.**

Do not forget this. We are in Christ. We are in the One Who is "Abraham's Seed." Because of this, we have received the promise of salvation according to God's promise "by faith alone!"

7

Galatians 4 (Part I)

Paul begins Galatians 4 by reminding us why we are no longer under the Law. In the previous chapter, Paul talked about the Law as being a schoolmaster and its purpose was to bring Israel to an understanding that righteousness through the Law is impossible. However, there is another reason and this time it has to do with us — the Body of Christ. Notice in the first verse there is mention of the word "heir." We are considered an heir to something that will be made plain as Paul continues. Galatians 4:1-2:

> 1 **Now I say, That the heir, as long as he is a child, differeth nothing from a servant, though he be lord of all; 2 But is under tutors and governors until the**

time appointed of the father.

Here, in this example, Paul uses a child who is an heir to something. We know that heirs receive their inheritance upon the death of someone, usually a parent, or upon attaining a certain age. However, while the heir is a minor, he or she must be looked after by tutors and governors. They carefully tend to the upbringing of the child. In wealthy homes it is very normal to have a governess for the children while they are young and a trustee to administer any assets held for the heir.

We can see from reading the passage that the context concerns the Law. The heir needs to be trained in a certain behavior and knowledge before inheriting the position of sonship. That is how it is under the Law. Paul is making the point here that when we were an unknowing child, we were under the Law being taught. Paul compares being a lost or unsaved person as being under the Law to that of being a child. Verses 3-4:

> 3 **Even so we, when we were children, were in bondage <u>under the elements of the world</u>:**

4 But when the fulness of the time was come, God sent forth his Son, made of a woman, made under the law,

While we were children, we were under the Law. Paul tells us that we were under "the elements of the world." What does this mean? Colossians 2:8-10:

8 Beware lest any man spoil you <u>through philosophy and vain deceit, after the tradition of men, after the rudiments of the world</u>, and not after Christ.

9 For in him dwelleth all the fulness of the Godhead bodily. **10** And ye are complete in him, which is the head of all principality and power:

Staying in Colossians, go to verses 2:20-22:

20 Wherefore if <u>ye be dead with Christ from the rudiments of the world</u>, why, as though living in the world, are ye subject to ordinances,

21 (Touch not; taste not; handle not; 22 Which all are to perish with the using;) after the commandments and doctrines of men?

So, the "elements" or "rudiments" of the world, which Paul refers to in Galatians 4, are explained here in Colossians. He calls the elements of the world weak and beggarly and, therefore, we should not be in bondage to them. He instructs us not to try to enter into a right relationship with God through the Law or get blessings from God through the Law. We cannot gain favor with God by keeping the commandments or ordinances. The model citizen who never breaks the law gets no benefit. However, if a citizen breaks the law, then there are consequences. Before understanding grace, we were in bondage to the elements of the world. We were in bondage to the Law.

It is clear that Paul is speaking about Jesus Christ when he tells us God sent forth His Son Who was made of a woman and made under the Law. What does he mean when he writes "but when the fulness of the time was come?" God has perfect timing. It was according to Daniel's prophecy concerning the appearance of Israel's Messiah. (See Daniel 9.) God sent His Son for what reason? Galatians 4:5:

> 5 **To redeem them that were under the law**, that we might receive the adoption of sons.

God sent His Son to redeem or buy back those that were under the Law. Those who were under the Law were Israel. The schoolmaster was to bring Israel to an understanding that righteousness does not come from keeping the Law. Paul makes the purpose for the Messiah's earthly ministry clear in Romans 15:8:

> 8 **Now I say that Jesus Christ was a minister of the circumcision for the truth of God, to confirm the promises made unto the fathers:**

Who are the *fathers?* They are Abraham, Isaac, and Jacob, who would later become known as Israel.

In Galatians 4, Paul uses the words *tutor* and *governor* to refer to training of the heirs who are children. However, once we have faith in Christ, we are no longer under the Law and have no need for the tutor or governor. We become adults in the gospel by faith. Galatians 4:6-7:

> 6 And because ye are sons, God hath sent forth the Spirit of his Son into your hearts, crying, Abba, Father.

> 7 Wherefore thou art no more a servant, but a son; and if a son, then an heir of God through Christ.

Here we begin to see the unique relationship created for those who are heirs by faith in the gospel. At the moment we believed the good news of salvation by grace through faith, we received the Spirit. The word *Abba* is similar to our word *Daddy!* Having accepted the truth of His gospel, we are no longer a servant. We have received sonship and, as such, we are heirs of God through Christ. Verses 8-9:

> 8 Howbeit then, when ye knew not God, ye did service unto them which by nature are no

gods.

9 But now, after that ye have known God, or rather are known of God, how turn ye again to the weak and beggarly elements, whereunto ye desire again to be in bondage?

Paul makes another comparison between the past and the present. He starts with "when ye knew not God" and continues with "but now" which reflects our present state. He says that the Galatians knew God or rather they were known by God. He turns that into a question concerning their change in belief. They have turned back to the weak and beggarly elements described below. By returning to the Law, Paul is asking them if they want to be in bondage again. To what sort of bondage is Paul referring? Paul continues by giving them an example. Verse 10:

10 Ye observe days, and months, and times, and years.

Can you think of a group of people who observe days, times, and years, and holy observances? That is Israel who is under the Law of

Moses. We need to understand that the Dispensation of Grace cannot be found in the Gospels. Israel was still under the Law. That is the reason that Christ was sent to redeem those under the Law so that we Gentiles might receive the adoption of sons.

The phrase "the adoption of sons" deserves some examination. Sonship is not something we can attain on our own. Here, we are not talking about natural sonship. We are talking about a spiritual *position* that God gives us through faith in Jesus Christ's finished work on the Cross. The moment we believe the Gospel we are then put in the *position* of being a full-grown son. We do not earn it. It is not the natural sonship, but rather it is given to us by God through faith in the Gospel of Grace.

Scripture clearly teaches that sonship is something we are given as part of our inheritance. Sonship is a position we receive at our salvation. It is immediate. Sonship has no gender. It cannot be received naturally as through a parent. We cannot attain it ourselves. It is a position similar to the Prince of Wales who is traditionally the heir to the throne of the United Kingdom. Let us look at some verses to add greater meaning to this. We will start with the Gospel of John. I understand that the Gospel of John is not specifically speaking to the current dispensation, but it does make the point in a general way concerning sonship. John 1:11-12:

> 11 **He came unto his own, and his own received him not.**
>
> 12 **But as many as received him, to them gave he power to become the sons of God, even to them that believe on his name:**

Christ came to His Own people. (See Romans 15:8.) The Jewish people were both male and female. So, sonship is not gender-based. It is spiritual. It is a spiritual possession. Now, let us go to Romans 8:14:

> 14 **For as many as are led by the Spirit of God, they are the sons of God.**

Paul writes "for as many as are led by the Spirit of God." They are what? They are "the sons of God." So, if we are being led by the Spirit, then we are a son of God. In other words, when we believe the gospel, being now led by the Spirit, we are the sons of God.

We continue. Verses 15-17:

15 **For ye have not received the spirit of bondage again to fear; but ye have received the Spirit of adoption, whereby we cry, Abba, Father.**

16 **The Spirit itself beareth witness with our spirit, that we are the children of God:**

17 **And if children, then heirs; heirs of God, and joint-heirs with Christ; if so be that we suffer with him, that we may be also glorified together.**

We are waiting for our glorification which is the final step of our adoption. This is when we receive our glorified body. Philippians 3:20-21:

20 **For our conversation is in heaven; from whence also we look for the Saviour, the Lord**

Jesus Christ:

21 Who shall change our vile body, that it may be fashioned like unto his glorious body, according to the working whereby he is able even to subdue all things unto himself.

The word *conversation* means *position*. So, our position is in heaven. Christ is in heaven and we are positionally *in Christ* presently although our fleshly bodies remain on earth. In the future, we are going to receive our glorified body like that of our Savior Jesus Christ.

Paul speaks about our earthly bodies. Romans 8:18-19:

18 For I reckon that the sufferings of this present time are not worthy to be compared with the glory which shall be revealed in us.

19 For the earnest expectation of the creature waiteth for the manifestation of the sons of God.

We become the sons of God when we believe the Gospel, but the manifestation of the sons of God is in future. That is when we receive our glorified body. Paul tells us about the final phase of our sonship. Romans 8:20-25:

> 20 For the creature was made subject to vanity, not willingly, but by reason of him who hath subjected the same in hope,

> 21 Because the creature itself also shall be delivered from the bondage of corruption into the glorious liberty of the children of God.

> 22 For we know that the whole creation groaneth and travaileth in pain together until now. 23 And not only they, but ourselves also, which have the firstfruits of the Spirit, even we ourselves groan within ourselves, waiting for the adoption, to wit, the redemption of our body.

> 24 For we are saved by hope:

but hope that is seen is not hope: for what a man seeth, why doth he yet hope for? 25 But if we hope for that [which] we see not, then do we with patience wait for it.

We started under the Law being constrained by our spiritual condition when we were in our fallen and sinful nature. However, once we received sonship, we know that we will be delivered from the bondage of corruption. We will enter into the glorious liberty of God's sons and daughters. We look with hope and confidence towards the future when we will be received by our Lord. Our physical body will be transformed into our glorified body. That is the completion of our adoption.

We will continue with the remainder of Galatians 4 in the next chapter.

8

Galatians 4 (Part II)

At the end of the previous chapter, Paul was concerned that the Galatians, after having received the glorious Gospel of Grace, had returned to the weak and beggarly elements. They were putting themselves back under bondage to the Law. We continue. Galatians 4:11:

> 11 **I am afraid of [for] you, lest I have bestowed upon you labour in vain.**

Paul is afraid they are bringing the Law into their walk with the Lord. It is a poor testimony for someone who claims to be saved by the gospel that Paul preached. Here, the word "lest" is translated "for fear that." He worries about them and their testimony. He also fears that his labors in teaching and preaching to them may have been futile. He wonders if the time he invested in them to establish them in the gospel was a waste of time. Did they really understand the Gospel of Grace at all?

Let us move on. Verse 12:

12 Brethren, I beseech you, be as I am; for I am as ye are: ye have not injured me at all.

So, what is going on here? Let us jump ahead. Galatians 5:13-15:

13 For, brethren, ye have been called unto liberty; only use not liberty for an occasion to the flesh, but by love serve one another.

14 For all the law is fulfilled in one word, even in this; Thou shalt love thy neighbour as thyself.

15 But if ye bite and devour one another, take heed that ye be not consumed one of [by] an-

other.

If we are operating under or walking in the Spirit, then we love our neighbor as ourselves and we love our brothers and sisters in Christ. If we are in the flesh and put ourselves back under the Law, what is going to happen? We are going to bite and devour one another. We are going to consume one another. I believe here the word "consume" means "to diminish, use up, or judge" each other according to the Law. Galatians 4:13-14:

> 13 **Ye know how through infir-mity of the flesh I preached the gospel unto you at the first.**
>
> 14 **And my temptation which was in my flesh ye despised not, nor rejected; but received me as an angel [messenger] of God, even as Christ Jesus.**

When Paul first came to Galatia to preach the gospel, they knew the imperfections of his human nature. Even knowing those weaknesses, they received him as a messenger of Jesus Christ Himself. The message he brought was the Gospel of Grace given to him which he delivered to them. In other words, when they looked at Paul, they looked at him with love, charity, kindness, and patience. They did not care about the problem with his eyes—his infirmities of his flesh. Verses 15-16:

> 15 Where is then the blessedness ye spake of? for I bear you record, that, if it had been possible, ye would have plucked out your own eyes, and have given them to me.

> 16 Am I therefore become your enemy, because I tell you the truth?

The physical problem he mentions could have been his issue with his eyes or some other physical problem. Regardless of what it was, Paul was received well by the Galatian assemblies. Now, he writes them as a chastising father would his children because they had put themselves back under the Law. Is he now their enemy for telling them the truth in love? So, what happened here?

The Judaizers had come into the assemblies and caused problems. They were telling the Grace Believers that it was not enough to believe the gospel. They also needed to observe the Law. Verses 17-18:

> 17 **They [the Judaizers] zealously affect you, but not well; yea, they would exclude you, that ye might affect them.**
>
> 18 **But it is good to be zealously affected always in a good thing, and not only when I am present with you.**

The Judaizers were zealous. They wanted to distance themselves from the Grace Believers so that they would not be affected by them. Paul wants the Galatians to remain zealous for the Gospel of Grace.

There was another possible reason the Galatians were adding the Law to the Gospel of Grace. It was out of fear of persecution from the Judaizers. Look at Galatians 6:12:

> 12 **As many as desire to make a fair shew in the flesh, they constrain you to be circumcised; only lest they should suffer**

persecution for the cross of Christ.

The Judaizers *constrain,* which means *to compel or to force,* the Galatians to be circumcised according to the Law. They were doing this *lest,* which means *for fear that,* they would suffer persecution. Why do they fear them? The Grace Believers did not want to be persecuted by "the circumcision" which are the Jews.

Paul looks forward to rejoining his Galatian brothers and sisters in fellowship. He desires to change his tone of voice from one of concern to one of confidence in their perseverance of the faith. Galatians 4:19-20:

> 19 **My little children, of whom I travail in birth again until Christ be formed in you,**
>
> 20 **I desire to be present with you now, and to change my voice; for I stand in doubt of you.**

Paul has great affection for the Galatian church and calls them "my little children" even though their position in Christ is full-grown sons. When they believed the gospel, they were automatically put in the position of being sons of God. However, their immaturity has caused them to be affected by outsiders. Paul continues to diligently work with them to correct this doctrinal problem until Christ be formed in them.

Paul continues to hammer home his point. Verse 21:

21 **Tell me, ye that desire to be under the law, do ye not hear the law?**

Paul asks the Galatians a question. Those of you who desire to be under the Law, do you understand what the Law is? When someone mixes law and grace, they neither understand law nor grace. Paul is about to provide the Galatians with a rebuttal to the Judaizers or, perhaps, this allegory was written for the Judaizers. All of Paul's epistles were intended to be read aloud in the assembly. The Jews are very familiar with the Old Testament. For them to comprehend the difference between Law and grace, Paul uses an allegory in verses 22 to 31. This was the manner of teaching Christ used in parables when teaching the Jews.

The symbolism is based upon Genesis chapters 16 through 18. (See also Hebrews 11.) Paul uses this to point out the difference between receiving grace by a promise and trying to receive it through the works of the flesh. The analogy involves three adults: Abraham, Sarah his wife, and Hagar his wife's servant. It will also involve two sons: Ishmael who is the son of Abraham and Hagar, and Isaac who is the son of Abraham and Sarah.

Paul will show how Abraham and Sarah received a son according to the promise without works of the flesh. Verses 22-23:

> **22 For it is written, that Abraham had two sons, the one by a bondmaid, the other by a freewoman.**

> **23 But he who was of the bondwoman was born after the flesh; but he of the freewoman was by promise.**

The bondwoman, Hagar, was an indentured woman who was the handmaid to Sarah, the wife of Abraham. The story in Genesis records that God made Abraham a promise that he would have a son through whom the promise would continue. Time passed and yet there was no son. Sarah, his wife, told Abraham to sire a child through Hagar, her handmaid, and this produced a son named Ishmael. Choosing not to wait on God, they took matters into their own hands rather than just trusting that God would fulfill His promise to Abraham. Paul refers to this as an act of the flesh and not one of faith.

Later, through God's help, Sarah conceived and bore a son who was named Isaac. This could only have been accomplished by God because of the advanced age of both Abraham and Sarah. They needed to trust God that He would fulfill the promise for them. Abraham had stopped walking by faith and chose to do a work of the flesh to try to fulfill the promise himself. Paul uses this as a lesson. Verses 24-26:

> 24 **Which things are an allegory: for these are the two covenants; the one from the mount Sinai, which gendereth to bondage, which is Agar.**

> 25 **For this Agar is mount Sinai**

in Arabia, and answereth to Jerusalem which now is, and is in bondage with her children.

26 But Jerusalem which is above is free, which is the mother of us all.

For those who do not know what happened on Mount Sinai, it is the mountain upon which Moses received the Law. Paul refers to Hagar, Agar within the text, as Mount Sinai. Mount Sinai is also the place where the Hebrews pledged to be bound by the Law and its ordinances. Hagar, as the bondwoman, represents bondage to the Law. Jerusalem represents the city to which all Jews and their children are bound to that Law. Then, Paul introduces the Jerusalem which is from above — the heavenly Jerusalem. This heavenly Jerusalem which he calls "the mother of us all" is a reference to Sarah. The Jerusalem from above is a promise and a work of God completed by God. It is neither by Man nor of the flesh. It is free in both cost and labor because it is a gift of God–promised and delivered by Him. The coming Jerusalem is God fulfilling the promise He made to Abraham. We can see the comparison in this *allegory* which is a representation.

The new Jerusalem is made by God Himself. It was not by the works of any man. It is a promise to believing Israel. The promises we have, as members of the Body of Christ, are based upon faith in the work of God and not our own. Our salvation is a work completed by God; not our works. This point Paul is making to benefit the Galatians two ways. First, it is a defensive argument against the Judaizers. Second, it will also be heard by all who are in attendance, including any Judaizers, at the reading of Paul's epistle in the assembly.

The book of Genesis is a fascinating book and well worth anyone's time to read it in full. For our purpose, we will highlight only small portions of this book relative to our current study. Genesis 16:1-6:

> 1 **Now Sarai Abram's wife bare him no children: and she had an handmaid, an Egyptian, whose name was Hagar.**
>
> 2 **And Sarai said unto Abram, Behold now, the LORD hath restrained me from bearing: I pray thee, go in unto my maid; it may be that I may obtain**

children by her. And Abram hearkened to the voice of Sarai. 3 And Sarai Abram's wife took Hagar her maid the Egyptian, after Abram had dwelt ten years in the land of Canaan, and gave her to her husband Abram to be his wife.

4 And he went in unto Hagar, and she conceived: and when she saw that she had conceived, her mistress was despised in her eyes. 5 And Sarai said unto Abram, My wrong be upon thee: I have given my maid into thy bosom; and when she saw that she had conceived, I was despised in her eyes: the LORD judge between me and thee.

6 But Abram said unto Sarai, Behold, thy maid is in thy hand; do to her as it pleaseth thee. And when Sarai dealt hardly with her, she fled from her face.

Prior to this, God had made a promise to Abraham that all the earth would be blessed through him, but yet Sarah continued to remain barren. Wanting that promise to be fulfilled, they decided to take matters into their own hands — a work of the flesh — to fulfill the promise. They had waited ten years for a child and then took action on their own. Abraham and Sarah acted in the flesh to fulfill a promise made by God.

Now, let us look at Genesis 17:15-16:

15 And God said unto Abraham, As for Sarai thy wife, thou shalt not call her name Sarai, but Sarah shall her name be.

16 And I will bless her, and give thee a son also of her: yea, I will bless her, and she shall be a mother of nations; kings of people shall be of her.

God had promised Abraham a son through Sarah. Verses 17-21:

17 Then Abraham fell upon his

face, and laughed, and said in his heart, Shall a child be born unto him that is an hundred years old? and shall Sarah, that is ninety years old, bear? 18 And Abraham said unto God, O that Ishmael might live before thee!

19 And God said, Sarah thy wife shall bear thee a son indeed; and thou shalt call his name Isaac: and I will establish my covenant with him for an everlasting covenant, and with his seed after him.

20 And as for Ishmael, I have heard thee: Behold, I have blessed him, and will make him fruitful, and will multiply him exceedingly; twelve princes shall he beget, and I will make him a great nation.

21 But my covenant will I establish with Isaac, which Sarah shall bear unto thee at this set time in the next year.

In spite of Abraham and Sarah's action, God still had a plan which He would fulfill Himself. Genesis 18:11-15:

11 Now Abraham and Sarah were old and well stricken in age; and it ceased to be with Sarah after the manner of women.

12 Therefore Sarah laughed within herself, saying, After I am waxed [grown] old shall I have pleasure, my lord being old also? 13 And the LORD said unto Abraham, Wherefore [Why] did Sarah laugh, saying, Shall I of a surety bear a child, which am old?

14 Is any thing too hard for the LORD? At the time appointed I will return unto thee, according to the time of life, and Sarah shall have a son. 15 Then Sarah denied, saying, I laughed not; for she was afraid. And he said, Nay; but thou didst laugh.

Abraham and Sarah should have trusted in God. By faith they should have known that He would accomplish His promise. We see this picture of Israel and the people who put themselves under the Law. Like Abraham, they try to attain God's promises by works of the flesh and not by faith that God Himself will fulfill them.

Therefore in Galatians 4:26, Paul is speaking about the heavenly Jerusalem which is from above. It is symbolic because it represents God fulfilling His promise Himself. Hebrews 11:8-11:

> **8 By faith Abraham, when he was called to go out into a place which he should after receive for an inheritance, obeyed; and he went out, not knowing whither [where] he went.**
>
> **9 By faith he sojourned in the land of promise, as in a strange country, dwelling in tabernacles with Isaac and Jacob, the heirs with him of the same promise:**

10 For he looked for a city which hath foundations, whose builder and maker is God.

11 Through faith also Sara herself received strength to conceive seed, and was delivered of a child when she was past age, because she judged him faithful who had promised.

Did you notice that? The city which Abraham sought is built by God and not by Abraham or his descendants. This symbolism was definitely understood by the Jews. The promises we have as members of the Body of Christ are also promises that God will fulfill. Those promises are based upon our faith in the work of God and not our own works.

We return to Galatians 4:27:

27 For it is written, Rejoice, thou barren that bearest not; break forth and cry, thou that travailest not: for the desolate hath many more children than she which hath an husband.

Paul finishes his comparison of Sarah who was barren but now rejoices in God knowing she will be the mother of many. We, like Israel, are children of promise. Verses 28-29:

> 28 **Now we, brethren, as Isaac was, are the children of promise.**

> 29 **But as then he that was born after the flesh persecuted him that was born after the Spirit, even so it is now.**

There was and continues to this day contention between the two offspring of Abraham. The descendants of Ishmael persecute the descendants of Isaac. Verse 30:

> 30 **Nevertheless what saith the scripture? Cast out the bondwoman and her son: for the son of the bondwoman shall not be heir with the son of the freewoman.**

I would like us to go back to Genesis 21:9-13:

> 9 **And Sarah saw the son of Ha-**

gar the Egyptian, which she had born unto Abraham, mocking.

10 Wherefore she said unto Abraham, Cast out this bond-woman and her son: for the son of this bondwoman shall not be heir with my son, even with Isaac.

11 And the thing was very grievous in Abraham's sight because of his son.

12 And God said unto Abraham, Let it not be grievous in thy sight because of the lad, and because of thy bond-woman; in all that Sarah hath said unto thee, hearken unto her voice; for in Isaac shall thy seed be called.

13 And also of the son of the bondwoman will I make a nation, because he is thy seed.

God agreed with Sarah that Isaac the child of

promise and Ishmael the child of works must be separated. This is also symbolic of the animosity that exists today between those who are saved by faith and those who believe they will be saved by works.

Paul is speaking to the Jews who still hold to the Law which is bondage. This story of Abraham is a poignant story for Jews as Abraham is the father of Israel. The Jews found letting go of the Law difficult because it is what they had been taught. It would be no different than Christians attending a church where the pastor teaches that salvation is obtained by grace and maintained by good works. That was the problem with the Galatian church. Paul wanted to be sure that the doctrine or gospel being taught was not of man but of God only. It is all about God, His promises, and his work; not those of man. It is about faith in God's promises. Galatians 4:31:

> 31 **So then, brethren, we are not children of the bondwoman, but of the free.**

9

Galatians 5 (Part I)

Paul continues to build upon the lesson in the previous chapter. Galatian 5:1:

1 Stand fast therefore in the liberty wherewith Christ hath made us free, and be not entangled again with the yoke of bondage.

When he says *stand fast*, he is telling them to hold their ground — do not be swayed. The word *therefore* is a conclusion to what he discussed in Galatians 4. He is telling them to stand immovable in the liberty of grace. Liberty is freedom and that freedom was bought for us by Jesus Christ's death, burial, and resurrection. Stand fast in the liberty and do not become entangled with the bondage which is the Law. Verses 2-3:

> **2 Behold, I Paul say unto you, that if ye be circumcised, Christ shall profit you nothing.**
>
> **3 For I testify again to every man that is circumcised, that he is a debtor to do the whole law.**

If someone becomes circumcised according to the Law in order to receive the benefit from doing so, then Christ shall be of no benefit to them. The same applies whether it is circumcision or any other work of the flesh. If we add anything to the Gospel of Grace, then Christ shall profit us nothing. It is either all Christ or nothing at all. We have to choose which one it will be. If we add the requirement of works to what Christ has already completed for us, then we are saying His work on the Cross was not sufficient for our salvation. We know that is not true. This applies to water baptism or any other requirement for salvation. If Christ did not do at all, then we are still dead in our sins and our faith is in vain. (See 1 Cor. 15:12-17).

We continue. Verse 4:

4 Christ is become of no effect unto you, whosoever of you are justified by the law; ye are fallen from grace.

Did you see that? The words "you are fallen from grace" are pretty powerful words. Falling from grace has to do with apostasy. It is moving altering the truth by changing the gospel. If someone tries to be justified by the Law, in whole or in part, then they have moved away from grace. They have put themselves back under the Law. They are an apostate. They are a heretic. Many religions teach salvation includes struggling to be good, trying to keep the commandments, and trying to meet the standards imposed by their current religious leaders. They are teaching the opposite of grace and what Paul is teaching.

In my past, I was in a denomination that taught freewill. I still believe in freewill, but they also taught that someone could lose their salvation. They taught that any believer can be in Christ, but if they walk away from Him, they would no longer be in Christ. In other words, we can lose our salvation. Later, I was involved with a Pentecostal denomination for a while. They taught the same thing: it is possible for us to sin to the point where we are no longer in Christ. They would say if someone walks away from Christ, then they are no longer saved — they have "fallen from grace." Well, my friend, that is a real twisting and turning of this verse. When we believe in the finished work of Christ's death, burial, and resurrection we are saved . . . period. We were purchased by His blood. This means that we are His, regardless of our subsequent actions or beliefs. Paul is teaching the concept of eternal security in Christ.

Looking again at that verse. It makes the point that if we are going to seek justification by the Law, if we are going to seek salvation by our works, if we want to be justified by our performance, then we are no longer operating under grace. We have "fallen from grace." That is how one falls from grace. We fall or turn away from grace. However, that does not change the fact that when we first believed, we were saved by the finished work of Christ. We are His! We were bought by His blood. We belong to Him.

There is another aspect we should consider. Dr. Greene shared a story in his dissertation of attending a baptism at a conservative

Baptist church. The preacher made the statement, "We all know that we are saved by grace through faith without works" to which the congregation responded with a resounding "Amen!" Then, the preacher continued, "But, we also know that we must do good works to maintain that salvation." The popular verses used to reject salvation by grace alone comes from James' epistle. James 2:20:

> 20 **But wilt thou know, O vain man, that faith without works is dead?**

At first, this appears to be a valid challenge to grace without works. However, let us go to the beginning of James and read the salutation. Verse 1:1:

> 1 **James, a servant of God and of the Lord Jesus Christ, to the twelve tribes which are scattered abroad, greeting.**

Perhaps an appropriate question for someone raising that objection would be, "Which of the twelve tribes are you from?" However, when dispensationally considered, it is clear that this is part of the Jewish epistles. These were written to the Kingdom Believers to prepare them for the coming Tribulation. Therefore, it does not apply to the Dispensation of Grace.

Some denominational churches teach that Christ did most of the requirements for salvation. All they need to do is the rest to be on the safe side. Paul is teaching exactly the opposite. If the Galatians put themselves under a performance-based system, then they have "fallen from grace." The opposite of falling is standing. This brings us back to the beginning of this chapter where we are told to, "Stand fast therefore in the liberty wherewith Christ hath made us free" (v.1).

We continue. Galatians 5:5:

5 For we through the Spirit wait for the hope of righteousness by faith.

Paul contrasts two things: being "through the Spirit" and being "under bondage of the Law." We now have liberty in Christ and are waiting for something while in our current state. What is this something for which we are waiting? We, through the Spirit, are waiting by faith "for the hope of righteousness." Wait a minute. Do we not already have God's righteousness imputed to us? Yes, we do. God's righteousness was imputed to us as a gift the moment we believed. However, we wait in our earthly bodies which are not righteous. We wait for our glorified bodies. When Paul talks about waiting for "the hope of righteousness by faith," he is talking about us waiting for the day when we will receive our glorified bodies in the presence of Christ. Now, we have Christ's righteousness spiritually. We have hope for the day when we will have a glorified body like the resurrected Lord Jesus.

Our hope is for the fulfillment of God's work in us. We have already been justified fully. We are looking for the blessed hope which is the Rapture. Then, we will receive our glorified bodies and be in His presence forever. Presently, we "wait for the hope of righteousness by faith." It will not be the righteousness that is imputed to us through faith in the Gospel, but the righteousness we will possess because we will no longer sin. With our glorified bodies, we will no longer get sick and no longer grow old.

Let us move on. Verse 6:

6 For in Jesus Christ neither circumcision availeth any thing, nor uncircumcision; but faith which worketh by love.

Neither circumcision nor uncircumcision provide any benefit or advantage. Rather, we are to walk by faith in God's love knowing what He has done for us and the promises of what He will do. Look back at Galatians 3:11:

11 But that no man is justified by the law in the sight of God, it is evident: for, The just shall live by faith.

If we walk by faith in what God has done and will do, then we cannot put ourselves under the Law. Instead, we must operate under grace by faith.

We continue. Galatians 5:7-8:

7 Ye did run well; who did hinder you that ye should not obey the truth? 8 This persuasion cometh not of him that calleth you.

Paul asks the Galatians who it is that hinders them. Who are the ones who are causing you to change the gospel? He assures them the persuasion to corrupt the gospel is not coming from him. (See Gal. 1:6.)

Keeping with the same theme, he takes a different approach comparing false doctrine to leaven. Here is another reference that the Judaizers would recognize. Verses 9-10:

> **9 A little leaven leaveneth the whole lump.**

> **10 I have confidence in you through the Lord, that ye will be none otherwise minded: but he that troubleth you shall bear his judgment, whosoever he be.**

Jesus, when speaking to the Pharisees, used this same reference. Let us look at a couple verses.

Matthew 16:6:

> **6 Then Jesus said unto them, Take heed and beware of the**

leaven of the Pharisees and of the Sadducees.

Matthew 16:11-12:

11 How is it that ye do not understand that I spake it not to you concerning bread, that ye should beware of the leaven of the Pharisees and of the Sadducees?

12 Then understood they how that he bade them not beware of the leaven of bread, but of the doctrine of the Pharisees and of the Sadducees.

Mark 8:15:

15 And he charged them, saying, Take heed, beware of the leaven of the Pharisees, and of the leaven of Herod.

Luke 12:1:

1 . . . he began to say unto his disciples first of all, Beware ye

**of the leaven of the Pharisees,
which is hypocrisy.**

Jesus used the word *leaven* to refer sin which permeates the entire loaf of bread. It represents lies, hypocrisy, and false doctrine.

Let us repeat the text. Galatians 5:9-10:

9 **A little leaven leaveneth the whole lump.**

10 **I have confidence in you through the Lord, that ye will be none otherwise minded: but he that troubleth you shall bear his judgment, whosoever he be.**

Most of us know what leaven is. The word *leaven* is a reference to *yeast*. Yeast is what we put in the dough to make the dough rise before it is cooked. It expands the dough. When leaven is mixed with the dough, it permeates the dough and causes the whole lump to expand and grow bigger. Most religious Jews would recognize the reference. Exodus 12:15:

**15 Seven days shall ye eat un-
leavened bread; even the first
day ye shall put away leaven
out of your houses: for whosoever eateth leavened bread
from the first day until the sev-
enth day, that soul shall be cut
off from Israel.**

The Lord commanded Israel to not eat
leaven. In fact, it must be cleaned out from
their houses. Why? The Lord views leaven as
sin and corruption. Those that disobey will be
cut off from their people. Another one of Paul's
epistles uses the word leaven. Look at 1 Corinthians 5:7-8:

**7 Purge out therefore the old
leaven, that ye may be a new
lump, as ye are unleavened.
For even Christ our passover is
sacrificed for us:**

**8 Therefore let us keep the
feast, not with old leaven, neither with the leaven of malice
and wickedness; but with the
unleavened bread of sincerity
and truth.**

In other words, leaven is like a poison when it is mixed into the Body of Christ. It only takes a spark to get a fire going that can then consume the whole. Sin and leaven, therefore, are viewed as the same thing.

Paul uses the same analogy, but in a slightly different way. In one situation, the leaven represented immorality in the Corinthian church. In the Galatian churches, the leaven is the people coming in and persuading the believers to put themselves back under the Law. Remember, a little leaven affects the whole. Paul is confident the Galatian church can put this behind them. Those who caused the problem, the Judaizers, will be judged by God.

We continue. Galatians 5:11-12:

11 **And I, brethren, if I yet preach circumcision, why do I yet [still] suffer persecution? then is the offence of the cross ceased.**

12 **I would [wish] they were even cut off which trouble you.**

Many are offended that Christ's death, burial, and resurrection is sufficient without works. Why? It is because they believe their works play a valuable part in their salvation. Their works of righteousness distinguish them from others. However, it is a biblical fact: salvation is offered to everyone who will believe in the complete work of Christ on the Cross. Unfortunately, to the self-righteous, this is offensive!

We will continue with Galatians 5 in the next chapter.

10

Galatians 5 (Part II)

Many Christians have been taught to keep the Law. They hold to their religious traditions, customs, and vain teachings of men and not God's Word. They believe their righteous acts count for something. All people, not just the Jews, are corrupt, wicked, and unrighteous. For that reason, God sent his Son. He became sin for us and shed His blood in payment of our sins. Why? There was nothing that man could do for himself. The condition of mankind is so bad, so desperate, so pathetic, so wicked that the only way they could be saved was by an act of God Himself.

It was Jesus Who completed the necessary work on the Cross. This single act allowed Him to say, "It is finished." Therefore, it is our faith in this gracious act of God that allows us to receive His righteousness. For those who strive for righteousness on their own through their own works, this is offensive.

Concerning the Judaizers who troubled the Galatians, Paul writes, "I would they were even cut off which trouble you." The word *would* is similar to the current *wish* or *would have it.* The words *cut off* mean *physical separation* from his people and the blessings of the covenant. It can also mean *eternal separation.* I do not believe Paul was wishing they would die. Nevertheless, he desired that those who trouble the Galatians would somehow be removed from the fellowship.

Many times, in our Christian life, the question arises as to what extent we should interact with non-believers. This especially applies to those who are promoting a false teaching or doctrine. Here are my thoughts on this issue. First, if they have a clear testimony of salvation, then we must treat them as our brother or sister even if we disagree with them. We are never to hate another person, but instead care about everyone. However, we cannot fellowship with anyone who is a non-believer on a spiritual level. We cannot be yoked to them. In our everyday lives we must interact with non-believers. Sometimes, we interact with people who profess to be believers and have a clear testimony of salvation. However, they believe or promote what is contrary to sound doctrine. From them, we must depart from having spiritual fellowship. They should be, to use Paul's wording, *cut off* from spiritual fellowship.

Let us move on. Galatians 5:13:

13 For, brethren, ye have been called unto liberty; only use not liberty for an occasion to the flesh, but by love serve one another.

Paul tells us that we "have been called unto liberty." To what "liberty" is Paul referring? If we look back to the beginning of this chapter, we see that Paul writes, "Stand fast therefore in the liberty wherewith Christ hath made us free." Liberty is freedom from restriction. For that reason, Paul continues with "and be not entangled again with the yoke of bondage." During the Jerusalem meeting, there were Judaizers there. (See Galatians 2.) Paul wrote, "that because of false brethren unawares brought in, who came in privily to spy out our liberty which we have in Christ Jesus." What was the purpose of these Judaizers? Paul continues the verse, "that they might bring us into bondage" (Gal. 2:4). Notice the comparison here between liberty which they have in Christ and these outsiders who wanted to bring them under the bondage of the Law.

We continue. Verses 14-15:

14 For all the law is fulfilled in one word, even in this; Thou shalt love thy neighbour as thyself.

15 But if ye bite and devour one another, take heed that ye be not consumed one of another.

Paul tells us that all of the Law can be fulfilled in one word: Love. How are we to do that? The ultimate expression of love, God's way and not the world's way, is through charity.

Charity is the key word Paul uses when he talks about love. 1 Corinthians 13:4-7:

4 Charity suffereth long, and is kind; charity envieth not; char-

ity vaunteth not itself, is not puffed up, 5 Doth not behave itself unseemly, seeketh not her own, is not easily provoked, thinketh no evil;

6 Rejoiceth not in iniquity, but rejoiceth in the truth; 7 Beareth all things, believeth all things, hopeth all things, endureth all things.

These are examples Paul gives in his letters to Grace Believers. He describes how love is to be expressed. When we practice this, we will not give into the flesh and worldly acts of self-serving. Love, instead, is selfless, self-sacrificing, and kind. It puts the needs of others above those of oneself. That is what Paul means by charity.

How are we to love those in Christ? Certainly, it is not biting and devouring one another to the point of destroying our brothers and sisters in Christ. This happens when we bring the Law into the fellowship. We judge each other according to the Law. We put ourselves under a performance-based system. We have certain expectations of ourselves and others. Then, there is no charity. There is no love. Paul tells us how we are to prevent this. Galatians 5:16-18:

> 16 This I say then, Walk in the Spirit, and ye shall not fulfil the lust of the flesh.

> 17 For the flesh lusteth against the Spirit, and the Spirit against the flesh: and these are contrary [against] the one to the other: so that ye cannot do the things that ye would.

> 18 But if ye be led of the Spirit, ye are not under the law.

We cannot serve God and, at the same time, walk in the flesh. We must walk in the Spirit. To bring glory to Him, we must be walking in the Spirit. If we do, then we will see the fruits of the Spirit manifested in our life. We can only walk in the Spirit by faith in God's Word and, particularly, God's Word rightly-divided. Colossians 2:6-7:

> 6 As ye have therefore received Christ Jesus the Lord, so walk

ye in him:

7 Rooted and built up in him,
and stablished in the faith, as
ye have been taught, abounding therein with thanksgiving.

So, when we receive Jesus Christ as our Savior
by faith, we receive the Spirit of God. It is not
something for which we hope or something we
will receive someday. We have the Spirit of
God now.

The Spirit is our assurance of our completed salvation. Ephesians 1:13-14:

13 In whom ye also trusted, after that ye heard the word of
truth, the gospel of your salvation: in whom also after that ye
believed, <u>ye were sealed with
that holy Spirit of promise,</u>

14 Which is the earnest of our
inheritance <u>until the redemption of the purchased possession,</u> unto the praise of his
glory.

The word "earnest" is an old legal term still used in real estate transactions today. Again, as we discussed before, it means "something given or done in advance as a pledge or security that guaranties the completion of a promise." We were purchased by the blood. The Spirit is the earnest Who guaranties the redemption of the purchased possession.

The Galatians had believed the Gospel of Grace delivered by Paul. They received eternal salvation and the Spirit of Promise as a guaranty. They had eternal security. However, having received their salvation by grace through faith alone, they now wanted to bring in the requirements of the Law. Keeping the Law is a work of the flesh. There are people all over the world who profess to be Christians. They are trying to earn their salvation by bringing their flesh under subjection to the Law. How can this save them or keep them saved? This is not something new. Isaiah spoke to the remaining two tribes. Isaiah 64:6:

> 6 But <u>we are all as an unclean thing,</u> and <u>all our righteousnesses are as filthy rags;</u> and we all do fade as a leaf; and <u>our iniquities, like the wind, have</u>

taken us away.

Isaiah lived more than 700 years before the birth of Christ. This pursuit of self-righteousness by works has not changed!

Paul makes a point about our position in Christ. If we have received Jesus Christ as our Savior and believed the Gospel, then we have the Spirit in us and we are also in Him. So, that is a position we now have. Since we have this position of being in the Spirit, we need to walk in the Spirit and not in the flesh. Paul lists some of the works of the flesh. Galatians 5:19-21:

> 19 **Now the works of the flesh are manifest, which are these; Adultery, fornication, uncleanness, lasciviousness,**
>
> 20 **Idolatry, witchcraft, hatred, variance, emulations, wrath, strife, seditions, heresies,**
>
> 21 **Envyings, murders, drunkenness, revellings, and such like: of the which I tell you before, as I have also told you in time past, that they which do**

such things shall not inherit
the kingdom of God.

I would like you to notice something at
the beginning of the next verse. It starts with
the word "but" because a contrast is made with
the preceding verses. Verses 22-23:

> 22 But the fruit of the Spirit is
> love, joy, peace, longsuffering,
> gentleness, goodness, faith, 23
> Meekness, temperance: against
> such there is no law.

Paul tells the Galatians that those who walk in
the Spirit will produce the fruit of the Spirit. By
doing this, it will prevent them from walking
in the flesh. Verse 24:

> 24 And they that are Christ's
> have crucified the flesh with
> the affections and lusts.

This is a positional truth. What do I mean
by that? Romans 6:1-2:

> 1 What shall we say then? Shall
> we continue in sin, that grace
> may abound?

2 God forbid. How shall we, that are dead to sin, live any longer therein?

In Romans, Paul makes the point that positionally, as Grace Believers, we are dead to sin — as far as God is concerned. Therefore, we are dead to sin. That is our *position*. Our identity is in Christ. Verses 3-6:

3 Know ye not, that so many of us as were baptized into Jesus Christ were baptized into his death?

4 Therefore we are buried with him by baptism into death: that like as Christ was raised up from the dead by the glory of the Father, even so we also should walk in newness of life.

5 For if we have been planted together in the likeness of his death, we shall be also in the likeness of his resurrection:

6 Knowing this, that our old man is crucified with him, that

the body of sin might be destroyed, that henceforth we should not serve sin.

We need to see this. There are two things going on here. First, we must see our *position*. Second, we must see our *practice*. We are in the Spirit and, therefore, we must walk in the Spirit. We are dead to sin. We are baptized into Christ's death, burial and resurrection when we believed the Gospel of Grace. We are not talking about water baptism. This is a spiritual baptism. This spiritual baptism is the likeness of His death and resurrection. We are in Christ. That is our *position*.

Now, what about our *practice?* Our old nature is like an old man who is crucified with Christ. This sinful man, our old self, is dead. As a result of this, we have a choice to no longer serve sin. Through the *practice* of not serving sin or giving in to sin, we acknowledge that we are dead to sin. Our *practice* is a continuing battle between our flesh and the Spirit. Our sin nature was crucified with Him. We must remember our *position* as we *practice* our walking in the Spirit.

Paul closes with these words. Galatians

5: 25-26:

> **25 If we live in the Spirit, let us also walk in the Spirit.**

> **26 Let us not be desirous of vain glory, provoking one another, envying one another.**

Paul is teaching that our *position* should affect our *practice*. Look at verse 25. It is a conditional statement. Here is the condition, "If we live in the Spirit . . ." In the event we meet that criteria, the result will apply, then ". . . let us also walk in the Spirit." Each of us who is saved by grace through faith should ask ourselves the question, "Are we walking in the Spirit?"

11

Galatians 6 (Part I)

Paul ended Galatians 5 with the theme of brotherly love. He continues by providing practical applications we can use as we learn to both "live in the Spirit" and "walk in the Spirit." Galatians 6:1:

> 1 **Brethren, if a man be overtaken in a fault, ye which are spiritual, restore such an one in the spirit of meekness; considering thyself, lest thou also be tempted.**

Paul begins with the words "Brethren, if a man be overtaken in the fault, ye which are spiritual." What does the phrase "ye which are spiritual" mean? We will see that it is directly connected to what Paul wrote in Galatians 5.

What are the characteristics of someone who is "spiritual?" We will find the answer here. 1 Corinthians 2:9-11:

> **9 But as it is written, Eye hath not seen, nor ear heard, neither have entered into the heart of man, the things which God hath prepared for them that love him.**
>
> **10 But God hath revealed them unto us by his Spirit: for the Spirit searcheth all things, yea, the deep things of God.**
>
> **11 For what man knoweth the things of a man, save the spirit of man which is in him? even so the things of God knoweth no man, but the Spirit of God.**

So, to be "spiritual," the Spirit of God reveals things to us about God that only the Spirit knows.

How does the Spirit reveal these things to us? He uses the Word of God. Verse 12:

12 Now we have received, not the spirit of the world, but the spirit which is of God; that we might know the things that are freely given to us of God.

How do we know the things that are freely given to us by God? Again. they are written down for us in His Word. Verse 13:

13 Which things also we speak, not in the words which man's wisdom teacheth, but which the Holy Ghost teacheth; comparing spiritual things with spiritual.

What is the standard for judging whether something is spiritual or not? We know that there is only one objective standard. This is the Holy Word of God. It is through the Word that the Spirit communicates to us. Continue with verses 14-15:

14 But the natural man receiveth not the things of the Spirit of God: for they are foolishness unto him: neither can he know them, because they

are spiritually discerned.

**15 But he that is spiritual judg-
eth all things, yet he himself is
judged of no man.**

Here is our answer! Paul tells us "he that is
spiritual judgeth all things." So, how does he
who is "spiritual" judge all things? Well, the
spiritual person has the standard by which he
may judge all things. What is the standard? Going back to verse 13, we see "the spiritual person judges all things by the Word of God."
Verse 16:

**16 For who hath known the
mind of the Lord, that he may
instruct him? But we have the
mind of Christ.**

How do we have the mind of Christ?

We have His Word revealed to us by the
Holy Spirit Who teaches us the mind of Christ.
We can know the mind of Christ through His
Word. Then, by faith, we are to put what we
know into practice. We are to exercise the mind
of Christ. How are we to do that? Consider this.
Philippians 2:1-4:

1 If there be therefore any con-
solation in Christ, if any comfort of love, if any fellowship
of the Spirit, if any bowels and
mercies,

2 Fulfil ye my joy, that ye be
likeminded, having the same
love, being of one accord, of
one mind.

3 Let nothing be done through
strife or vainglory; but in lowliness of mind let each esteem
other better than themselves.

4 Look not every man on his
own things, but every man also
on the things of others.

When we have the mind of Christ, we understand the Word of God. Then, we put it into
practice through our attitudes and actions towards other members of the Body of Christ.
How?

We do this by esteeming our brothers
and sisters in Christ better than ourselves. Not
serving our own needs alone, but also ser-

ving the needs of others. Verses 5-8:

> 5 **Let this mind be in you,
> which was also in Christ Jesus:**
>
> 6 **Who, being in the form of
> God, thought it not robbery to
> be equal with God:**
>
> 7 **But made himself of no repu-
> tation, and took upon him the
> form of a servant, and was
> made in the likeness of men:**
>
> 8 **And being found in fashion
> as a man, he humbled himself,
> and became obedient unto
> death, even the death of the
> cross.**

Therefore, being "spiritual" is putting the mind of Christ into action in our life. Just as Christ did by humbling himself, we are to have a selfless and self-sacrificing attitude. That is how we are "spiritual."

Therefore, we know that "he who is spir-itual" is someone having the mind of Christ. We get this from God's Word. There is a deeper concept that needs to be included here. 1 Corinthians 14:37:

> **37 If any man think himself to be a prophet, or spiritual, let him acknowledge that the things that I [Paul] write unto you are the commandments of the Lord.**

Being "spiritual" means acknowledging the things that Paul wrote are God's instructions for the Age of Grace. The significance of these commandments of God which Paul received are for this current dispensation. Peter, James, and John wrote for Israel. Their writings apply to the Kingdom Gospel. That is an important difference! Therefore, a believer who is "spiritual" will rightly-divide the Word of Truth and will understand that Paul wrote for the Dispensation of the Grace of God.

When interacting with fellow believers, the "spiritual' believer must practice charity by exercising meekness and humbleness. In regards to someone who was "overtaken in a fault," Paul instructs us to restore them "in the spirit of meekness" and not through arrogance or superiority. He says we should do this while "considering thyself." What does he mean by that?

At some point in time, every believer makes a wrong decision and, as a result of that, could be caught in the snare of the Devil. Let us look at 2 Timothy 2:24-26:

> 24 **And the servant of the Lord must not strive; but be gentle unto all men, apt to teach, patient,**
>
> 25 **In meekness instructing those that oppose themselves; if God peradventure will give them repentance to the acknowledging of the truth;**
>
> 26 **And that they may recover themselves out of the snare of the devil, who are taken captive by him at his will.**

This servant of the Lord about which Paul is speaking would be a "spiritual man." Paul is telling us to instruct with lowliness of stature those who oppose themselves. How do people oppose themselves? That would be someone who acts against their best interest by contending or fighting with the Spirit. They are going against the Spirit Who is acting in their best interest.

Now, let us move on. Galatians 6:2:

> 2 **Bear ye one another's burdens, and so fulfil the law of Christ.**

What is the law of Christ? Here are some characteristics for interactions with other members of the Body of Christ. Romans 12:14-18:

> 14 **Bless them which persecute you: bless, and curse not.** 15 **Rejoice with them that do rejoice, and weep with them that weep.**
>
> 16 **Be of the same mind one toward another. Mind not high things, but condescend to men of low estate. Be not wise in your own conceits.**
>
> 17 **Recompense to [Repay] no man evil for evil. Provide things honest in the sight of all**

men. 18 If it be possible, as much as lieth in you, live peaceably with all men.

In the whole chapter of Romans 12, Paul lists character traits that each Christians should have when interacting with others. Like Christ, we are to love others, not as we love ourselves, but rather as Christ loved us. Remember, He died for us out of love and He loves us no less today.

We continue. Galatians 6:3:

3 For if a man think himself to be something, when he is nothing, he deceiveth himself.

Contrary to "the spirit of meekness," we think that we are something special or, in other words, we are puffed up. We are actually nothing and only deceive ourselves. How does this tie in with what we are talking about here? It is important we keep this in mind. In our study, Paul has an overriding theme throughout his letter to the Galatian assemblies. It all starts with faith: believing the Gospel of Grace as Paul presented it. The Judaizers falsely taught that observing the Law was a requirement of salvation. By doing this, it would help believers to receive blessings and favor from God. Keep this in mind as we bring this study to an end. We read "if a man think himself to be something, when he is nothing, he deceives himself" (v. 3). If they believe themselves to be wiser than Paul's teachings, then they are nothing. They deceive themselves.

How should we interact with other believers? Romans 12:1-5:

> 1 I beseech you therefore, brethren, by the mercies of God, that ye present your bodies a living sacrifice, holy, acceptable unto God, which is your reasonable service.
>
> 2 And be not conformed to this world: but be ye transformed by the renewing of your mind, that ye may prove what is that good, and acceptable, and perfect, will of God.
>
> 3 For I say, through the grace given unto me, to every man that is among you, not to think

**of himself more highly than he
ought to think; but to think so-
berly, according as God hath
dealt to every man the measure
of faith.**

**4 For as we have many mem-
bers in one body, and all members have not the same office: 5
So we, being many, are one
body in Christ, and every one
members one of another**

Paul teaches that every man should not think
of himself more highly than he ought to think.
If anyone does, then they deceive themselves.
The Judaizers, who by haughtiness of thought,
sowed error in the Galatian assembly. They
were overriding Paul's gospel which he received from the Risen Lord. Unfortunately,
many Christians think they are superior in
knowledge or purity than others. They teach
things outside of God's Word because of their
haughtiness or arrogance. Well, according to
Paul, they deceive themselves.

Consider this. 2 Corinthians 10:12:

12 For we dare not make our-

**selves of the number, or com-
pare ourselves with some that
commend themselves: but they
measuring themselves by
themselves, and comparing
themselves among themselves,
are not wise.**

Here, Paul discusses the issue of judging others by comparing someone else's spirituality to themselves. This may be either by appearance or some other measure. Usually they make themselves the measure by which they judge others. Paul gives his response. 1 Corinthians 10:12:

**12 Wherefore let him that
thinketh he standeth take heed
lest he fall.**

Here we see it again. There has always been an issue with people who, through arrogance and lack of humility, think they stand as examples. They end up falling. The deceive themselves.

We return to Galatians 6:4-5:

**4 But let every man prove his
own work, and then shall he**

**have rejoicing in himself
alone, and not in another.**

**5 For every man shall bear his
own burden.**

Each of us is accountable to God. It is important to know that we are not talking about salvation. We are talking about the receiving or losing of rewards. When we read "let every man prove his own work," we are talking about holding ourselves accountable. We are to measure our own actions by comparing them to Scripture and not comparing them to others. Again, we are to qualify our own actions and not those of others. When we think about the words *prove* and *work*, one biblical verse comes to mind. Let us look at 2 Timothy 2:15:

> **15 Study to shew thyself approved unto God, a workman that needeth not to be ashamed, rightly dividing the word of truth.**

One day we will stand before the Lord Jesus Christ and we will be asked to provide an accounting on the basis of how we served Him. Each believer will be answerable. Every believer must prove his own work by comparing it to Scripture. If we rightly-divide the Word of Truth, then we will not be ashamed for misinterpreting God's Word. If we know in our heart that we are doing what God has instructed us to do, then we can rejoice in our own works.

We continue. Verse 6:

> 6 **Let him that is taught in the word communicate unto him that teacheth in all good things.**

The above verse is not easy to understand. Let us focus on the word *communicate*. Look at another place Paul uses the same word. Philippians 4:12-17:

> 12 **I know both how to be abased, and I know how to abound: every where and in all things I am instructed both to be full and to be hungry, both to abound and to suffer need.**
>
> 13 **I can do all things through Christ which strengtheneth me.** 14 **Notwithstanding ye**

have well done, that ye did communicate with my affliction.

15 Now ye Philippians know also, that in the beginning of the gospel, when I departed from Macedonia, no church communicated with me as concerning giving and receiving, but ye only.

16 For even in Thessalonica ye sent once and again unto my necessity. 17 Not because I desire a gift: but I desire fruit that may abound to your account.

What is Paul talking about here? It sounds like he is talking about supporting the ministry or making an offering. Now, let us look at 1 Timothy 6:17-19:

17 Charge them that are rich in this world, that they be not highminded, nor trust in uncertain riches, but in the living God, who giveth us richly all things to enjoy;

18 That they do good, that they be rich in good works, ready to distribute, willing to communicate;

19 Laying up in store for themselves a good foundation against the time to come, that they may lay hold on eternal life.

Here, the word "charge" is similar to the charge given at the installation of officers. It is both a challenge and a warning to those being installed. We do not get the impression that Paul is speaking only about money. Yes, he does mention the giving of material things. It is important to do what we can do support the ministry of the Gospel of Grace.

Paul will continue on this subject in the next chapter.

12

Galatians 6 (Part II)

We are continuing with the remainder of Galatians 6. Let us start by repeating Galatians 6:6:

6 Let him that is taught in the word communicate unto him that teacheth in all good things.

In other words, if we are taught in the Word by those who are teaching us all good things, then we need to show them support. When we support the teachers of the Word rightly-divided, which is the teaching of sound doctrine, we support the doctrine being taught. It means that we are in agreement with what God is doing today. We support it by either our material gifts or by sacrificing our time. Verses 7-9:

7 Be not deceived; God is not mocked: for whatsoever a man soweth, that shall he also reap.

8 For he that soweth to his flesh shall of the flesh reap corruption; but he that soweth to the Spirit shall of the Spirit reap life everlasting.

9 And let us not be weary in well doing: for in due season we shall reap, if we faint not.

Paul has not moved on to another subject. When he writes "communicate unto him that teacheth in all good things," he is instructing us to support those who teach sound doctrine. We share in their work. We mock God when we think we are getting away with something. Do you remember that the overall theme of Galatians concerns those who are trying to place Grace Believers under the Law? They put themselves under the Law and, therefore, they put themselves under judgment as well. That is sowing to the flesh. That is going off the rails. However, supporting the ministry of right doctrine is sowing to the Spirit. The reward for the latter is reaping from the Spirit everlasting life.

Notice that the consequence of the fleshly approach to salvation is corruption. In Scripture, the word *corruption* is associated with death: both physical death and the absence of spiritual life which is eternal. Here is an example that confirms much of the content in the previous verses. Romans 8:5-6:

> **5 For they that are after the flesh do mind the things of the flesh; but they that are after the Spirit the things of the Spirit.**

> **6 For to be carnally minded is death; but to be spiritually minded is life and peace.**

We must understand that Paul is writing to those who are already saved. If we believe the gospel that Christ died for our sins, was buried, and rose on the third day, then we are sealed by the Holy Spirit until the day of Redemption. We are placed completely under God's grace by faith in what Christ did for us on the Cross. We cannot lose our salvation. We were bought and paid for by His blood.

Paul is teaching that those who allow their minds to be outside the truth, allowing in false teaching and being carnally-minded, leads to death in the sense of an absence of spiritual life. They are not walking in the truth God has given. On the other hand, being spiritually-minded there is life and peace. Having freewill, the choice is ours. Verses 7-8:

> 7 Because the carnal mind is enmity against God: for it is not subject to the law of God, neither indeed can be.
>
> 8 So then they that are in the flesh cannot please God.

Paul's theology is consistent whether it is from Galatians or Romans. Let us finish our comparison. Verses 9-13:

> 9 But ye are not in the flesh, but in the Spirit, if so be that the Spirit of God dwell in you. Now if any man have not the Spirit of Christ, he is none of his.
>
> 10 And if Christ be in you, the body is dead because of sin; but the Spirit is life because of

righteousness.

11 But if the Spirit of him that raised up Jesus from the dead dwell in you, he that raised up Christ from the dead shall also quicken your mortal bodies by his Spirit that dwelleth in you.

12 Therefore, brethren, we are debtors, not to the flesh, to live after the flesh. 13 For if ye live after the flesh, ye shall die: but if ye through the Spirit do mortify the deeds of the body, ye shall live.

Paul's points are clear. We should not be carnally-minded. We should not try to live our Christian lives through the flesh by trying to keep the Law in order to obtain salvation. This leads to corruption which is spiritual death. However, if we live through the Spirit and not according to our fleshly desires, then we have life and peace. Paul teaches about those who live by the Spirit in 1 Corinthians 15:42-44:

42 So also is the resurrection of the dead. It is sown in corrup-

tion; it is raised in incorruption: 43 It is sown in dishonour;
it is raised in glory: it is sown
in weakness; it is raised in
power:

44 It is sown a natural body; it
is raised a spiritual body.
There is a natural body, and
there is a spiritual body.

Paul makes four comparisons in the above
verses: corruption-incorruption, dishonor-
glory, weakness-power, and natural-spiritual.
Corruption, dishonor, weakness, and the natural body all lead to death. While incorruption,
glory, power, and a spiritual body are all refer-
encing eternal life.

Now, we are going to tie this important
subject together. 1 Corinthians 15:50-58:

50 Now this I say, brethren, that
flesh and blood cannot inherit
the kingdom of God; neither
doth corruption inherit incorruption.

51 Behold, I shew you a mys-

tery; We shall not all sleep, but
we shall all be changed,

52 In a moment, in the twin-
kling of an eye, at the last
trump: for the trumpet shall
sound, and the dead shall be
raised incorruptible, and we
shall be changed.

53 For this corruptible must put
on incorruption, and this mortal must put on immortality.

54 So when this corruptible
shall have put on incorruption,
and this mortal shall have put
on immortality, then shall be
brought to pass the saying that
is written, Death is swallowed
up in victory.

55 O death, where is thy sting?
O grave, where is thy victory?
56 The sting of death is sin; and
the strength of sin is the law. 57
But thanks be to God, which
giveth us the victory through
our Lord Jesus Christ.

58 **Therefore, my beloved brethren, be ye stedfast, unmoveable, always abounding in the work of the Lord, forasmuch as ye know that your labour is not in vain in the Lord.**

Anytime Paul repeats something, our attention should be drawn to the subject. However, it takes some study to see that what he taught on a subject, as important as this, is in multiple letters. His point is that corruption and death go hand in hand. Being fleshly or carnally-minded, for example believing false doctrine, leads to corruption which leads to death. Those who teach false doctrine to others, like leaven, expands the corruption. However, walking in the Spirit by following Scripture leads to life and peace. Supporting a ministry that teaches right doctrine, whether materially or physically, leads to life and peace.

We return to our text. Galatians 6:7-8:

7 Be not deceived; God is not mocked: for whatsoever a man soweth, that shall he also reap.

8 For he that soweth to his flesh

shall of the flesh reap corruption; but he that soweth to the Spirit shall of the Spirit reap life everlasting.

Here are two examples. Those who smoke cigarettes are going to smell bad, frequently get sick, and possibly die early from cancer. If we eat poorly and do not exercise, then it could result in obesity, diabetes, and heart problems. They may become sick and die. They are hurting themselves, right? When someone behaves poorly, they physically reap what they sow. This can also apply to the spiritual as well. There too we reap what we sow spiritually.

Paul applies this concept to the Judaizers in the Galatian assembly. Those who communicate or teach bad doctrine — false teaching — are sowing corruption and that corruption leads to death. Those who accept false teaching will reap the same corruption because of these false teachers. If we believe the Gospel of Grace, then we already have eternal life. We have everlasting life. However, there is a practical application for those who have eternal life. That is living like someone who has eternal life. When we are spiritually-minded, we support and contribute to the teaching of sound doctrine.

We continue. Verses 9-10:

9 And let us not be weary in well doing: for in due season we shall reap, if we faint not.

10 As we have therefore opportunity, let us do good unto all men, especially unto them who are of the household of faith.

Spiritually, we must continue doing what we know is right from the Scriptures and, one day, we will reap a good harvest. We should live in the Spirit by doing the right thing, believing correct doctrine, and working to further the Gospel. We can do that materially, financially, and by encouraging those that teach the Word rightly-divided. The Law of Christ is to do good to all; specially to love and care for our brothers and sisters in Christ. This *is not* the Mosaic Law. This *is* the Law of Christ which is the Law of Love. It is easily fulfilled by letting the Spirit lead us. Verse 11:

11 Ye see how large a letter I have written unto you with

mine own hand.

Galatians is one of the few letters that Paul actually wrote with his own hand. For most of his letters he used an amanuensis or scribe to take dictation or to copy an original manuscript to make duplicates. It is generally understood that Paul's eyesight was poor. For that reason, he wrote with large letters.

The next verse is very interesting. Verse 12:

> **12 As many as desire to make a fair shew in the flesh, they constrain you to be circumcised; only lest they should suffer persecution for the cross of Christ.**

Paul is referring, again, to these Judaizers who have come into the Galatian assemblies. The word "constrain" means "to compel by physical, moral, or circumstantial force." What were the Galatian believers being compelled to do? The Judaizers wanted them to be circumcised according to the Law. Why were they doing this? The word "lest" means "for fear that." The Galatian believers felt compelled to be circumcised for fear that they would be persecuted by these Jews because of the Cross. The Cross represents Christ's death, burial, and resurrection which is sufficient to save. To the Jews, it is offensive because Christ fulfilled the Law. Their self-righteousness will avail them nothing. To avoid persecution by the other Jews, they compelled the Galatian believers to become circumcised. Again, they were mixing Law with grace, trying to appease the Pharisees, Sadducees, and other pious Jews so as to avoid persecution.

Moving on. Verse 13:

13 For neither they themselves who are circumcised keep the law; but desire to have you circumcised, that they may glory in your flesh.

These Judaizers are basically hypocrites. They fail to keep the Law themselves, but compel the others to be circumcised according to the Law. They do this so "that they may glory in your flesh." What does this mean? They want to be able to boast by saying, "See what we got the Gentile believer to do! We got them to keep the Law and become circumcised to receive God's blessing." When they have accomplished their purpose, then they glory in the flesh.

Paul gives his response, knowing he is being led of the Spirit. Verse 14:

14 But God forbid that I should glory, save [except] in the cross of our Lord Jesus Christ, by whom the world is crucified unto me, and I unto the world.

Paul is making a very strong statement. He is saying that anything that is added to salvation by grace through faith is of the flesh. All the religious stuff, putting someone back under the Law, or putting them under some kind of religious performance-based system is all worldly. If it is of the world, if it is of the flesh, then it is of Satan.

Religious rites and traditions are the tools the Satan uses to counterfeit and corrupt God's Word. Worldly religion wants us to think we can be saved by doing something. That is corruption of the Gospel of Grace. That is of the world. That is of the flesh. Paul finds the concept of self-aggrandizement repulsive saying, "God forbid that I should glory." All he chooses to glory in is "the Cross of our Lord Jesus Christ." He then professes that he is dead to the world and the world to him. This is the best example of living in the Spirit.

We continue. Verse 15:

15 For in Christ Jesus neither circumcision availeth any thing, nor [does] uncircumcision, but a new creature.

Whether we are circumcised or not, it is of no value spiritually. Instead, we are saved by believing in Christ's death, burial, and resurrection. Grace Believers are a new creature in Christ. Recall Paul's words. Galatian 3:28:

28 There is neither Jew nor Greek, there is neither bond nor free, there is neither male nor female: for ye are all one in Christ Jesus.

Whether someone is circumcised or not is a non-issue for the Grace Believer. We are the Body of Christ. We are one in Christ. Therefore, making distinctions between believers is a corruption of Scripture. It is a worldly view; not spiritual. 2 Corinthians 5:15-17:

> **15 And that he died for all, that they which live should not henceforth live unto themselves, but unto him which died for them, and rose again.**

> **16 Wherefore henceforth know we no man after the flesh: yea, though we have known Christ after the flesh, yet now henceforth know we him no more.**

> **17 Therefore if any man be in Christ, he is a new creature: old things are passed away; behold, all things are become new.**

We did not know Christ during his earthly ministry to Israel as some did. Those that did know Him during His earthly ministry know Him no more in the flesh. Paul concludes with "Therefore, if any man be in Christ, he is a new creature." What are the distinguishing factors of this new creature? The "old things are passed away and all things are become new."

We learn from the Corinthian epistle that we are a new creature "in Christ." We are no longer a Jew following the Law or a Gentile following man-made religions. For us, those things have passed away and everything has become new. Now, let me pose a question. Can that be said about our personal life? For us, have all things become new? What God is doing today with the Body of Christ is totally different from anything that He has done before. It is totally new — spiritually speaking.

Paul continues. Galatians 6:16:

16 And as many as walk according to this rule, peace be on them, and mercy, and upon the Israel of God.

This blessing refers to the preceding verses in which we are told that none should glory except in the Cross of our Lord Jesus Christ. Paul concludes Galatians like a father who has finished chastening his children. Verse 17:

17 From henceforth let no man trouble me: for I bear in my body the marks of the Lord Jesus.

What does Paul mean by this? Let us go to another reference where Paul makes remarks about his body. Colossians 1:24:

24 Who now rejoice in my sufferings for you, and fill up that which is behind of the afflictions of Christ in my flesh for his body's sake, which is the church:

Paul is not comparing his suffering with those of Christ. He is saying he is made to suffer for the message Christ gave him. Verse 25:

25 Whereof I am made a minister, according to the dispensation of God which is given to me for you, to fulfil the word of God;

He takes upon himself the suffering for the Body of Christ and the message he brings. It is for that reason he writes to "fill up that which is behind the afflictions of Christ in my flesh." The "body's sake" of which Paul speaks is the Church—the Body of Christ. Paul has suffered and will continue to suffer until his execution in Rome. He is doing all this to teach the Gospel of Grace. When he wrote, "henceforth let no man trouble me," I believe he was saying, "Enough of this. I have gone to great lengths to explain that the Gospel cannot be altered and those that do so are accursed." During his life, Paul had sacrificed much for the presentation and preservation of the message to which God had entrusted him.

Paul finishes his scolding with words similar to "don't let this happen again." He reminds the Galatians of "the grace of our Lord Jesus Christ" by which they have freely received their salvation. We all have hope because the Holy Spirit dwells within us. The holy Spirit of Promise is the guaranty of the final redemption of our bodies. However, until then, we are to walk in the Spirit. Verse 18:

> 18 **Brethren, the grace of our Lord Jesus Christ be with your spirit. Amen.**

Other GraceWord Publications

In English:

1st Corinthians: Dispensationally Considered
1st & 2nd Thessalonians: Disp. Considered
1st & 2nd Timothy & Titus: Disp. Considered
2nd Corinthians: Dispensationally Considered
Acts: Dispensationally Considered
Colossians & Philemon: Disp. Considered
Ephesians: Dispensationally Considered
Galatians: Dispensationally Considered
Hebrews: Dispensationally Considered
How Am I Wired?
Letters To Theophilus
Philippians: Dispensationally Considered
Romans: Dispensationally Considered
The Glorious Destiny Of Israel
The Gospel of John: Disp. Considered
The Gospel of Luke: Disp. Considered
The Gospel of Mark: Disp. Considered

The Gospel of Matthew: Disp. Considered
The Hidden Gospel
The Seven Hebrew Epistles: Disp. Considered
Two Distinct Gospel Messages Of The N.T.

En español:

Cartas A Teófilo
Efesios: Dispensacionalmente considerado
El evangelio Oculto: Una vez fue un misterio

About The Author

Steve Tackett is a well-known teacher, conference speaker, pastor, and evangelist with over thirty-five years of experience. He is the retired president of Grace Bible Network which produced weekly radio broadcasts and online classes.

His passion is teaching the Word of God rightly-divided. He has a uniquely adaptive teaching style which allows beginner students as well as seasoned Grace-Believers to understand and enjoy their Bible. He places the Bible in its rightful place of authority using Scripture to teach Scripture. This simple approach teaches anyone interested in understanding the Bible how to search and understand the Bible on their own.

His expositional teaching presents the Bible with an emphasis on Paul's message of the Gospel of the Grace of God.